I0069763

'Sameer possesses the innate ability to tap into arch[...]
forged by centuries of habit, and transform them into p[...]
nisms that prepare us for the future – without alienating us in the process.
It is rare for an innovator to also possess the gift of the common touch.'
– Pluto Panoussis, Co-Founder, Open Window
University for the Creative Arts, Lusaka

'I've known Sameer since childhood, and he has always been ahead of
his time. His creativity, wisdom and innovative ideas shine through in
everything he does. This book is a testament to his talent, and I'm
excited for readers to experience his unique perspective.'
– Juraj Hudak, Partnerships and Commercialization Lead,
Neom City, Saudi Arabia

'Sameer addresses relevant educational needs in a creative manner. He
is an effective problem-solver and system-thinker in an ever-changing
world.'   – Dr Karen Walstra, former Google for Education
Programme Manager, Sub-Saharan Africa Team

'Sameer has a way of seeing the world that blends wisdom and modern-
ity. He has a way of making unconscious truths, conscious. When you
read his work you feel like someone is speaking to the deepest parts of
your inner being.'
– Faheem Chaudhry, former M&C Saatchi Abel Managing Director
and Financial Mail AdFocus Awards Chairman

'Sameer explains AI like no other – giving an intelligent explanation of
where we stand with AI.'   – Ray White, Radio Host, Radio 702

'Sameer has a rare ability to see past conventional wisdom to unwrap
new perspectives and answers.'
– Jon Foster-Pedley, Dean, Henley Business School Africa

'Sameer is a literal visionary and a true leader, always aspiring to make the world a better place with greater equality.'
— Fizza Hasan, Digital Marketing Leader,
McKinsey & Company

'Sameer has an unlimited store of ideas that can improve the world, culture and the future.'
— Victor Udoewa, former Chief Technical Officer,
Chief Experience Officer and Service Design Lead, NASA

'His insights on technology can transform learning and development.'
— Evgeni Agronik, former EMEA Head of Ads Policy, Google

TAKING
THE ANXIETY
OUT OF AI

TAKING THE ANXIETY OUT OF AI

Humans, Economies and Jobs in the Age of Artificial Intelligence

SAMEER RAWJEE

PENGUIN BOOKS

Taking the Anxiety out of AI

Published by Penguin Books
an imprint of Penguin Random House South Africa (Pty) Ltd
Reg. No. 1953/000441/07
The Estuaries No. 4, Oxbow Crescent, Century Avenue, Century City, 7441
PO Box 1144, Cape Town, 8000, South Africa
www.penguinrandomhouse.co.za

Penguin
Random House
South Africa

First published 2025

1 3 5 7 9 10 8 6 4 2

Publication © Penguin Random House 2025
Text © Sameer Rawjee 2025

All rights reserved. No part of this publication may be reproduced,
stored in a retrieval system or transmitted, in any form or by any means,
electronic, mechanical, photocopying, recording or otherwise,
without the prior written permission of the copyright owners.

RESPECT CREATORS
SAY NO TO ILLEGAL COPYING

Making illegal copies of this publication, distributing them unlawfully
or sharing them on social media without the written permission of
the publisher may lead to civil claims or criminal complaints.

Protect the communities who are sustained by creativity.

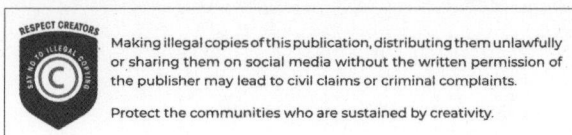

PUBLISHER: Marlene Fryer
MANAGING EDITOR: Robert Plummer
EDITOR: Christa Büttner-Rohwer
PROOFREADER: Dane Wallace
COVER AND TEXT DESIGNER: Ryan Africa
TYPESETTER: Monique van den Berg

Set in 12 pt on 16.5 pt Minion 3

Printed by **novus print**, a division of Novus Holdings

MIX
Paper | Supporting
responsible forestry
FSC
www.fsc.org
FSC® C022948

ISBN 978 1 77639 210 0 (print)
ISBN 978 1 77639 211 7 (ePub)

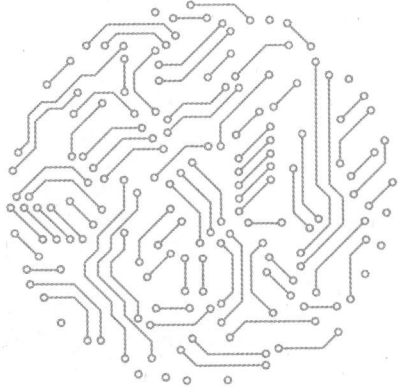

CONTENTS

The 'why': The story of life, humans and AI
Begin the conversation about where we currently are as
humans and move towards the technology aspect of the
conversation

The future in three lines

AI takes jobs
Customers want new experiences
Humans prevail again

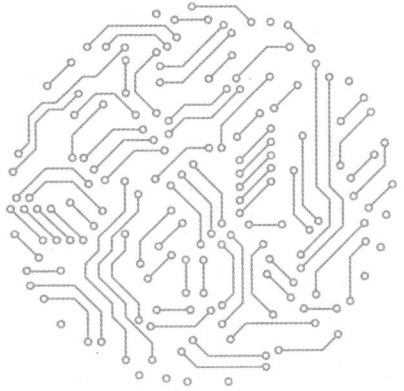

ABBREVIATIONS

AGI: artificial general intelligence
AR: augmented reality
CEO: chief executive officer
CIO: chief information officer
GDP: gross domestic product
GPT: generative pre-trained transformer
GPU: graphics processing unit
HR: human resources
IT: information technology
KPIs: key performance indicators
LLM: large language model
MECE: mutually exclusive, collectively exhaustive
ML: Machine learning
NLP: Natural language processing
ROI: return on investment
SaaS: Software as a Service
SDGs: Sustainable Development Goals
UBI: universal basic income

PART 1
HUMANS

To understand what a machine is, you have to understand what a human is. That is the only way you can know the difference between machine and human, and your place in a future society that is just around the corner.

WHAT MAKES
HUMANS HUMAN

In an episode of *Star Trek*, the USS *Enterprise* encounters a primitive planet inhabited by a peaceful, agrarian society that appears indifferent to the galaxy's conflicts. When the crew warns them of an impending Klingon invasion, they are shocked to discover that the inhabitants don't care about taking any precautions at all. Instead they insist on 'peace' being their approach to life. This baffles the crew, as it just doesn't make any sense. But when the Klingons arrive, expecting an easy conquest, they are effortlessly rendered powerless by the beings, who impose peace without lifting a finger.

It turns out that these beings are not primitive at all, but in fact one of the most advanced civilizations in existence. Long before, they transcended physical existence and chose to abandon technology and warfare, seeing them as distractions from evolution. They realized that technological advancement was not the answer to their problems and that instead of dabbling in superficial matters, they would explore a whole new reason for existence. After learning this, Spock from the *Enterprise* turns to his crew and says that these beings 'are as far above us in the evolutionary scale as we are above the amoeba'.

This is probably the same realization we will come to in 100 years' time. We're currently building super-advanced technology, not because it's needed, but because we can. Because we want to test our intelligence to the furthest degree. Despite some of the dangers of AI, we still revel in the prospect of playing god, whether as engineers, designers or entrepreneurs. We convince ourselves that we're producing ideas that people want to buy, but as Steve Jobs put it, 'people don't really know what they want until you show it to them'. Consumers don't have the headspace to ask deeper philosophical questions; they are just living out the story of advertising. So while it might look as though the flashy aspects of our world represent human progress, it's worth questioning what progress really means.

Trevor Noah put it simply, saying that a million years of evolution allowed us to develop an upright posture, and now that we spend every hour looking down at our phones, our gaze is becoming so low that we're turning into monkeys again. The brain and neural advances we've made are also deteriorating. With so many stimuli, we want to be everywhere at once. We want to be in every post, buy every gadget, read every article and invest in every stock. So it's hard to maintain a reasonable focus on any one thing, and this is causing us to naturally develop an acute attention deficit disorder. And without the ability to pay attention we cannot preserve our memory, and without memory we cannot access our knowledge. What does that make us then? No more than jellyfish floating through the ocean. This is what it means when the tech evolves but the people don't. We are not mentally, emotionally and spiritually advanced enough to coexist with what we create.

This is why China blocked US EdTech companies from providing Scholastic Aptitude Test (SAT) tutoring support in the country. They said that these services create such fierce competition among Chinese children that students are developing mental health disorders. More tutoring companies pop up each year promising the Ivy League dream, but the number of spots at Harvard and Columbia stays the same. It just doesn't make sense that these industries would even exist. But five years ago you might have thought, 'Wow, these smart entrepreneurs in Silicon Valley are building amazing tutoring companies, big brand-name venture capital firms are investing, and millions of customers are buying these products.' And, even if we intuitively knew that the website testimonials were of only three kids out of one million customers that actually got into Harvard, you'd still believe that these companies were building the future. Everything makes sense in retrospect. And so it is as though we have to get to the point where humans crash to realize that all of our thinking was actually flawed and driven by a state of awareness that did not consider the complete nature of the human.

We are in the process of creating a world where in some ways we will make major leaps and other ways we will just mess up. We have a deep curiosity to get to that place where we almost destroy ourselves so that we know we took the chance to create whatever we wanted. There seems to be a hope that we can keep pushing the needle, keep abusing ourselves and the environment, and maybe, just maybe, everything will still be okay. This is how a child tests the limits of life: by pushing the glass to the edge of a table, we slowly see how far we can go. We get to the point where the possibility of the glass falling is exceptionally high. But when we are five years old, we don't really know for sure. Sure, the destruction might be overwhelming, but the satisfaction of finally pushing it over the edge may fulfil us too. And so we are the children who have inherited the earth, finding out who we are and pushing the limits of our existence.

That's what AI is. A chance to see what we are and what we can be. A chance to play god, no matter the repercussions, economic impacts or societal dilemmas. And while most of the world will simply need to make the financial and educational leap as technology progresses, the best scientists and venture capitalists who are producing these technologies have already made that leap. They don't work for money anymore. Now they are just here to have fun, to see how far humans' capacity and intellectual prowess can go.

And while that might sound morose to most, it's humanity's best bet at survival; it's the push we need to find out who and what we really are.

WHAT IS A HUMAN?

For centuries, our best philosophers have had incredible ideas about what they think is uniquely human. Their works make for great reading in the evenings before bed and their ideas come up as beautiful reflections on a Sunday at church. But that's as far as they go, and as far as we go. Outside of that we remain in our primitive mindsets: we desire; we fear; we chase cash and beer; we follow routine and make sure our families have eaten. That's pretty much it. Nothing more, nothing less.

Sometimes we make deeper psychological leaps through a TED Talk, a TV show or a dream – but while that temporarily enlightens us, maybe for a few hours each year, we eventually default to our primitive habits. Humans could be so much more, but there just hasn't been any real motivation to evolve further.

Until now.

Why? Because in the mid-2020s we are realizing that machines will eventually be able to do almost everything we can do. So this is the time we are forced to find out whether we can be more than we have been, not as a matter of interest but out of necessity.

This will be the first time in secular society that people will talk about the human soul at work as a way to differentiate who we are from algorithms and hardware. The soul, which would have been considered a soft topic, now becomes an urgent topic as machines' rights are measured against our own or as machines' emotions are considered equal to ours during a workplace conflict. This may be the era in which you have to sit in a corner with your eyes closed to contemplate higher truths.

It will be the first time we will need to better differentiate between us and other animals on the planet. We might think we are more evolved than monkeys, but how we behave shows otherwise. As Elon Musk reminds us, our brains are fundamentally split into two parts: the limbic system and the cortex. The limbic system is the animal brain in you, focused on sex, food and survival, while the cortex focuses on higher functions such as critical analysis, imagination and problem solving. But so far most human behaviour stems from the limbic system, and the majority use of the cortex is in service of the limbic system. In other words, you get knowledge to get rich, to get resources, to attract more partners, to have more sex. So we are basically just higher-functioning animals. But if machines are not in service of such lower-order biological needs, does that mean that they have access to higher-thinking abilities or more advanced approaches to organizing life on earth? Maybe the answer is yes, but it is only yes until we evolve beyond our basic mammalian instincts.

This will also be the first time we will join together to support each other in new ways because, like aliens landing on the planet, it will be the first time there is an 'us versus them' mindset – humans versus machines. We may start looking at our fellow humans in a more unified way. The idea now is not just to build a world that is better for you and your family, but a world that services our unique human needs.

This is when all of humanity will ask, 'What makes me uniquely human now?' And that is a fine question, because it is the basis of evolution and the foundation on which our species will progress.

WHAT IS HUMAN INTELLIGENCE?

In his famous TED Talk titled 'Do schools kill creativity?', Sir Ken Robinson says that we have a very narrow view of human intelligence and as a result we do not educate the *whole human*. His talk has been watched 23 million times and is the third most watched TED Talk in history. While most viewers would have simply found it *refreshing*, it is probable that today those same people would find it *urgent*. This is because we only educate for intellectual intelligence, which can be largely replaced by machines over the next decade. But humans have, in fact, a combination of intelligences:

- **Intellectual**: Having the ability to reason, problem-solve and create new ideas.
- **Emotional**: Seeing your emotions as data and knowing what to do with them.
- **Physiological**: Knowing the relationship between your body and the world as a way to navigate it.
- **Intuitive**: Knowing a truth without evidence to make decisions or create new solutions.
- **Spiritual**: Knowing that you exist beyond your mind-made self and what to do with that wisdom.

What Robinson goes on to say is that 'I think math is very important, but so is dance. Children dance all the time if they're allowed to; we all do. We all have bodies.' But also, 'Truthfully, what happens as children grow up is that we start to educate them progressively from the waist up. And then we focus on their heads. And slightly to one side.' Which means we are missing out on educating a large part of what makes us human. In a way we have reduced education to preparing children just for left-brain thinking, i.e. maths and science, and that minute aspect of who we are and what we have trained for is exactly what machines can copy and eventually perform better than us.

Robinson then says, 'We need to radically rethink our view of intelligence. We think about the world in all the ways that we experience it. We think visually, we think in sound, we think kinaesthetically. We think in abstract terms, we think in movement.' So while AI wasn't nearly a topic of the times when he gave this talk in 2007, it's clear that these are fundamental principles on which we will now need to think of educating ourselves next. These will be the aspects of intelligence, and the interactions therein, that give us a place in a future where we coexist with machines.

SO WHAT IS 'ARTIFICIAL' INTELLIGENCE?

AI is just mimicking human intelligence, that's it. Our world's best scientists want to find out how to get computers to think like humans or become humans. The only problem is that different scientists have different ideas about what intelligence is. Some of them may not even consider Sir Ken Robinson's interpretation. They do not see humans in a multidimensional way but rather as mere cogs in a capitalist machine – in which case they believe they can recreate human-like forms with the entirety of human ability. They see humans as just intellectual machines with emotions as speed bumps.

Some will even say that emotions are our downfall and that's why machines are better than us. Moreover, if machines need to develop any emotional intelligence, then it is only to deal better with us or make us feel more comfortable around them. Other than that, machines don't need emotions or any of the other intelligences. To these scientists, the other intelligences merely provide insight on what makes us human and have no functional value in building a future run by robots.

Of course this understanding is very limited. It assumes that our intellect does not interact with nor is improved by our emotions, physical sensations and intuition – and vice versa. Rather it assumes intellect is some isolated activity that happens at its best without these other human functions. But many social scientists or philosophers or anthropologists would say otherwise. The problem is that the best computer scientists are sometimes not the best social scientists, and that promotes a development of machines that is incompatible with the best possible future for humans.

Moreover, a robot's intellectual abilities are also only based on existing human knowledge. Machines can only reflect the extent of human intelligence. Robots or chatbots take all of the existing human knowledge and then organize it in ways that help us answer the questions we have. 'We get what we feed' – which is kind of like 'we are what we eat'. But we are still creating new knowledge and learning about new ways to coexist, so our human story is not over; machines are merely helping us use our current information better, for now.

For example, the whole world needs therapy. And while the best therapy happens between people in real life, not everyone has a consistent group of friends or $150 a week for a therapist. So while a machine cannot give you everything you need, or the satisfaction of a human connection, it can certainly support your mental health journey. It can certainly predict a possible set of solutions based on your cognitive behavioural patterns, and it's free for the two billion people who need this help right now.

It is also worth saying that while machines can interpret your emotions by how you sound or speak – and even mimic emotions – they can never actually feel them. They are not biological beings with biological processes. Moreover, the other intelligences mentioned above are all interconnected with biological processes, so while they might be mimicked too, they cannot be experienced or accessed in the same way as humans access them. There is still something about us that is far superior to machines, and it will always be this way.

WHAT IS ARTIFICIAL GENERAL INTELLIGENCE (AGI)?

While today we have AI plugged into a great deal of the software we already use without us even knowing it, such as our phones giving us exactly the news we want, our Instagram feeds being highly tailored to our interests, and our emails predicting how we want to respond – and then there are apps that are overtly cutting-edge AI, such as ChatGPT – it is safe to say that AI is still in its nascent stages. It's like a baby who has just been born and will need to experience a great deal of growth before achieving fully functional adult maturity, knowledge and intelligence. And in the same way that it takes several decades for a human baby to fully mature, so it could take AI several decades to become the best version of itself. Technologists refer to this fully matured AI as artificial general intelligence or AGI – so it's worth knowing that when we talk about AI being as smart as humans we are talking about AI in its final form, which is called AGI. Some believe AGI will be the point at which we can't tell the difference between a human being and a robot by its looks, functioning and intelligence. But, as I said earlier, there are and will always be limits to this. Robots can mimic us, but can never be us. Robots can infer, but not intuit. Robots can create, but not imagine. Robots can recite a prayer, but not have mystical experiences. Robots can invent, but cannot come up with those magical visions you just *feel in your bones.*

Ray Kurzweil, chief AI visionary at Google, also says that we will soon reach *the singularity,* which means that we will reach a point where machines will far outperform humans. Does this mean they will be more intelligent than humans? The answer is both yes and no.

Yes, computers will be able to perform most tasks better than humans and may even have better ideas for organizing society than is already imagined. When you can see data from every angle, at rapid speed, against millions of models, you'll likely see things most humans never see or that would take humans decades to see. Creativity is sometimes this magical thing that happens as a dance with the universe but other times it's just reorganizing the same ingredients in a different way to come up with a new soup. And machines can probably imagine a thousand different soups per second. Without the sense of taste, it is hard to imagine that those soups would be any good, but surely a machine can come up with at least one good soup, never imagined before by a human. The same would be true for a piece of music, a strategy, a policy, a product or a manufacturing process.

But, on the other hand, intelligence isn't just reduced to out-performing humans on everyday tasks. We always have to ask higher questions such as: Why should we do this task anyway? Does this represent our values? Does this help us progress as a society? Will this make economic sense in five years? These questions require other forms of human intelligence. In addition, robots can create new knowledge but only ever on the data they have in their systems. So much new knowledge is often created by scientists dreaming into the abyss and asking questions such as 'Mmm, what if I mixed X with Y, would Z happen?'

This daydreaming is called intuiting, and this intuiting turns into hypotheses and hypotheses turn into science, which turns into knowledge. And this is all uniquely human.

Even so, machines and humans could together become a great force for futures that are unattainable through human ability alone. It's true that some nutty scientists sitting somewhere in California might think that it would be a great human achievement to let robots imagine and manage their own futures. These scientists want to see what would happen if robots were given control to do whatever they wanted to. It's what the co-founder of Google, Larry Page, implied when he said that robots may be better than humans, so why not let them do their own thing. But this is an entirely flawed idea, since it assumes robots are a life form, when really they are just glorified hammers and screwdrivers that are intended to always serve human needs.

WHAT ARE MACHINES FOR?

Firstly, what is a machine? It is just a tool to achieve a goal. It can be a drill, a washing machine, a phone, ChatGPT, or a robot that makes autonomous decisions about how to change the world. Whether that machine is just a white box that washes clothes or a white box with a face, voice and human body that understands emotional cues and tells you jokes while it washes, steams and folds your clothes is irrelevant. But because we are such visually oriented creatures, we usually become incredibly engrossed in what we see. So if a robot looks like a human, we will believe it is a human, and we will develop a relationship with the machine and infer ideas about it, such as whether it should have a religion, go to school or have marriage rights. And, for an irrational species like us, there is nothing wrong with that; let's just not forget that this is still just a washing machine dressed up like a doll.

Machines are simply here for one thing: to help humans achieve their goals. Some scientists have different ideas about this. They might say things like, 'Well, what if robots are a better species than us? Shouldn't they have a chance to evolve and take us over?' And the response to that is, to what end? What purpose does a machine have on earth without humans here? The answer is none.

Sure, if machines are more logical than humans, they might wipe us out to help the earth heal. But even without machines, humans could become extinct on their own or be forced to leave the planet at some point anyway, and then the earth will eventually replenish itself. The earth only takes a thousand years to return to its natural order – and then another species will have a chance to use our planet for its evolution.

But evolution is more than an intellectual activity – it's not only about becoming the 'smartest we can be', it is also a spiritual journey, says million-copy bestselling author Neale Donald Walsch. 'Our purpose is to know who we are by knowing who we are not.' And without getting too mystical, this could just mean that we are here to move from fear to love, understand the interconnectedness between us humans or become the best version of ourselves.

Perhaps, then, it is fair to say that machines are largely here to do all the grunt work for us, to make society more equitable, and to help with producing our goods and services so that we can move our attention to higher evolutionary needs. We can move up Maslow's hierarchy, as it were – and we can start focusing on other intelligences to become a better, collaborative and more unified species.

WHY ARE HUMANS HERE?

Eckhart Tolle, who wrote the 20-million-copy bestseller *The Power of Now* and also happens to be Oprah's favourite author, said it quite simply when describing the purpose of human existence: 'We are here to get to know who we are beyond our mind-made selves.' That's all. In other words, human existence is more than about getting a degree, pursuing a job and providing for your family. That would make this whole experience meaningless, or simply empty. Rather, there is something that exists beyond your name, your identity or your ego that you are here to experience too. The famous behavioural scientist Abraham Maslow would have called it *self-actualization*, but the cheeky British philosopher Alan Watts would simply call it *living*. Either way, human beings are here to contemplate something more than mere survival, more than just making it through from day to day.

But Tolle also provides a more material response to this question when he says that we also have an outer purpose. And that outer purpose is to use our talents and passions to help fellow human beings. Whether as an engineer or artist, writer or company director, you are here to use what makes your soul feel alive to create work that helps other people live better lives. You may be helping people with simple tasks such as getting a nicely brewed coffee in the morning to start their day with a smile, or maybe your job is to educate the kids of the future by being the most present teacher you can be. Or perhaps your job is to paint beautiful works that hang in public spaces and uplift the human spirit or record meditations on YouTube to help people make emotional leaps. Whatever it may be, each of us has some outer purpose to which we feel called, to move the world forward.

Our existence is also designed to help us to know each other better, and therefore ourselves better. So if machines take over our work and we sit at home building relationships with other machines, that defeats the purpose of our existence. We might get comfortable dating robots, getting therapy from a chatbot or having dinner with virtual characters, but soon we will yearn for human connection again. That's why the future isn't as bleak as it seems. Every time we make some technologically advanced leap, it seems that people still crave basic things again – markets for vintage goods are popular for that reason. We got MP3 players, now people want vinyls. We got smartphones, now tons of Silicon Valley execs are buying dumb phones to avoid distraction. We abandoned cinemas and got TikTok, now people crave long-form films again. And so the same will be true for the era we are about to enter next. Tech will be very beautiful and help us advance a lot, in many good ways. But the more machine-oriented and predictable things become, the more human connection and imperfection we will yearn for once again.

Commerce is also not just for commerce's sake: it gives us a chance to get to know each other. If we all had all the cash we needed from the start of human history, then we wouldn't be forced to leave our houses and engage with each other, have tough discussions, grow emotionally, and create new knowledge about ourselves and society. And while in current times it feels as though we could all use a two-year break from capitalism, if it were an option, we might soon find ourselves yearning to work again.

Why? Because commerce pushes us to deal with larger human issues. It forces us to work across global markets and therefore do business with different cultures. It forces us to share offices, and therefore most of our waking hours, with people we would otherwise never encounter. And it pushes us to talk about matters such as gender equality, women's empowerment, black leadership and indigenous progress – all because we are forced to achieve the same goals with different people. So while all of this is sometimes painful in the short term, it is actually amazing in the long run. We and newer generations crave for this progress, for this connectedness, and we are all better off as a result.

So, even if machines take over our current jobs, a part of

us will still be hungry for this growth. In ten years' time, when machines have taken all our basic jobs, and we all get a free basic income from the government, we will still want to solve new problems and create new opportunities. Life is not only about consuming products or chilling at home to play video games. We still want to have more discussions about how to live in a more peaceful and harmonious way. We still want to learn more about what we can become as a people – and this desire will drive future versions of the human story. AI is not where our humanity ends, it is where a new chapter for all of us begins.

MENTAL MODELS

At the end of each chapter I provide a mental models box. Here I present a set of summaries or ideas that are useful for you to keep in mind as a busy entrepreneur, executive or manager in the AI era. Think of these points as a way to keep the main ideas of this book in your mind, so you can draw on them in meetings, brainstorms or discussions around the future. Think of them as tools you can rely on to organize your thinking about AI in a simple way.

- **There are five types of intelligence**: intellectual, emotional, physiological, intuitive and spiritual. Robots will most likely only be able to master and surpass us in pure intellectual intelligence – problem solving and critical analysis. The other intelligences can be mimicked but not fully adopted by robots, because they are interconnected with specific human senses and biology. For example, a robot can make a guess from existing data but not have an intuition about the future.

- **There are three stages of AI development:** The first is *narrow AI*. These are AI tools designed to perform specific tasks – such as ChatGPT, where we can ask questions and get tailored answers. The second is *artificial general intelligence* or AGI. This is the point at which a robot can do anything a human can do (and it's still questionable whether this is completely possible) – it is the form of AI we see in Hollywood movies. And the third is *the singularity* – a situation in the future where robots have the freedom to talk to other robots and make their own goals and decisions without humans regarding how society is shaped. This may or may not be a doomsday scenario.

- **There is one fundamental truth about humans:** People will always want to connect with other people, so as long as we are around, no matter how far machines go to replace us in our jobs, we will always find new ways to congregate, do business and search for higher truths. There will always be new opportunities.

THE MIND
AND THE SOUL

In January 2019, US journalist Scott Pelley from the CBS News show *60 Minutes* interviewed 'the oracle of AI', Kai-Fu Lee – Taiwanese billionaire, computer scientist and co-author of the book *AI 2041*, published by Penguin in March 2024. This is a short snippet from their conversation:

Scott Pelley: So when can we expect machines to be smarter than humans?

Kai-Fu Lee: If you're talking about AGI, artificial general intelligence, I would say not within the next 30 years and possibly never.

Scott Pelley: Possibly never? What's so insurmountable?

Kai-Fu Lee: See, I believe in the sanctity of our soul; I believe there's a lot of things about us that we don't understand. I believe there's a lot of love and compassion that is not explainable in terms of neural networks and computational algorithms and I currently see no way of solving them. Obviously unsolved problems have been solved in the past but it would be irresponsible for me to predict that these will be solved by a certain time frame. We may just be more than our bits.

Is that true, or are humans just another machine? Well, a human is a type of machine, if analysed by its physical parts alone. We are electro*chemical* and machines are electro*mechanical*.

In short, this means that both robots and humans use electricity to send information throughout their bodies. Robots use batteries to generate electricity, whereas humans use food to create chemical energy, which is then converted into electrical signals.

Robots use electrical signals to control their movements across a *circuit*. The physical parts of a robot, such as metal arms and legs, are mechanical components. But humans use electrical signals to control their movements across the *nervous system*. The physical parts of a human, such as arms and legs, are organic components. So it would seem, then, to the simple-minded scientist, that machines and humans are exactly the same, only different *material*.

Hence the question, 'Are we more than just our bits?'

But this is where serious questioning ceases, maybe because this is where material evidence ends and philosophical questioning begins. Maybe these topics have traditionally been wrapped up in religious rhetoric, and religion isn't so popular anymore. But this doesn't mean we can't have logical conversations without subscribing to mystical ideas. Whether you are religious or not, if I ask you if you have a soul, your immediate inclination might be to say 'yes!', but then your mind comes in and questions what a soul is, whether you actually have one or whether you're lost in some lofty spiritual idea. Or perhaps you believe you have a soul but you don't really think about it that much, or you might not even care about whether you have a soul or not because you cannot see its relevance to your daily financial pursuits.

But in the age of superintelligent machines, where billionaires and computer scientists will claim that robots have souls too, and therefore equal rights to you, maybe only then you will be jolted out of your indifference to really question what that means or how you fit into that story. In the age of machines being able to do it all, it will be the things that differentiate us that will matter most. And very few things will differentiate us from machines as much as the human soul.

SO HOW DO YOU KNOW YOU HAVE A SOUL?

Almost every great philosopher, scientist and historical icon would have reflected on the higher ideas of being human, all the way from Kant to Maslow to Nelson Mandela. They all spoke of connecting with the soul as the pinnacle of human experience. Maslow called it self-actualization, while modern spiritual gurus such as Jay Shetty and Deepak Chopra would call it self-realization and some contemplative neuroscientists such as Sam Harris and Andrew Huberman would call it enlightenment – that which is achieved through simply entering the present moment.

It was in the early seventeenth century that the great French philosopher René Descartes first said, 'I think, therefore I am.' In other words, if you are thinking, then that must mean you exist, or rather that you exist because you are aware of yourself thinking. But then later, in the twentieth century, the philosopher Jean-Paul Sartre looked at this statement and thought that if there is an 'I' that is doing the thinking, then surely I exist beyond thought, surely there is something that makes me what I am before thought even happens. And that's obvious: if you *have* a thought, you can't *be* a thought. This also means you are not your mind, which is just the collection of your thoughts.

You are also not your body. You know this because you say you have a body, and you cannot *be* something that you *have*. And so if you are not your body or your mind, that must mean you are something else beyond those two things. You can be simple about it and say that you are just the awareness of your body and mind. That would not be inaccurate. Or you can give that awareness a name and call it your soul. That makes you a three-part being consisting of mind, body and soul. Not complicated or mystical or religious at all.

And if you don't want to use the word 'soul', then you know there is definitely something that is not the body and mind that exists and has life force. You know this when you see a patient who is brain-dead and therefore cannot use their mind: the body is there, but there is 'life' beyond that body, which is why you will think twice before you switch off the oxygen supply. And so, even if you just want to call it life force, what we know for sure is that you are more than what you appear to be. You are more than just your parts.

THE AGE OF SPIRITUAL MACHINES

In 1999 Ray Kurzweil, now chief AI scientist at Google, wrote a book called *The Age of Spiritual Machines*. In it he talks about what humanity would look like by 2045, which at the time seemed unthinkably far in the future. But many of his ideas have been realized in the past 20 years and, as we make the next 20-year leap, it seems valuable to revisit some fundamentals.

In his book, Kurzweil uses the word *spiritual* liberally, so the deeper question is what is spirituality anyway? The practice of spirituality is simply about connecting with your true nature. Without making the matter too complicated, this means that if you close your eyes and focus on your breath, then you create space between you and your thoughts, and when you do this, you find some inner space to experience some inner peace – and that's all that humans really want at their core. Too often we are lost in thought and that makes life very difficult. Almost every human lands up at one predictable realization after a long period of difficulty, and that realization is 'I just want some peace of mind'. While the average human means that they want their problems to go away when they say this, meditation, a tool that helps us create that inner space, is now quickly becoming a vital practice in a world where everyone needs inner peace, no matter their outer life situation.

And while a ten-minute meditation at lunch is often enough to feel some relief from your anxiety before you get back to work, some people sit in silence for hours or even months. Yuval Harari, author of *Sapiens*, is known to spend two months a year at a Vipassana meditation retreat, where, for 60 days, he will simply be in silence. He says it helps him think clearly and organize his mind. Tons of research from institutions such as Stanford and Harvard also show that meditation improves problem solving, creativity, focus, relationships and social dynamics. And mystics who spend several hours a day in meditation, throughout their whole lives, say that sitting in that space may also lead to mystical experiences, where we transcend to something well beyond our senses.

However, Ray Kurzweil says that advanced AI will appear to have free will and 'claim to have spiritual experiences' too, and that people will believe this. But of course a machine cannot 'find space beyond its mind'. It may look, feel and think like a human being, but it is not human, and can never be.

So those benefits of meditation, which is a practice of spirituality, will probably become very useful when attempting to calculate, solve or see things that machines cannot see. Maybe this is what

Einstein meant when he said, 'I want to know the mind of God, the rest are details.' A machine may have a faster mind, but it cannot meditate its way above its mind; therefore we will always have the potential for a more brilliant mind – a machine cannot be more than its parts.

WHEN WILL MACHINES BE CONSCIOUS?

This is currently a major question for scientists and philosophers alike. While it is one of the most fascinating topics of our era, what most people understand as 'conscious' or 'consciousness' differs vastly. First, they mean different things but are often used interchangeably by people who do not know the difference between them. And that's not their fault; we are talking about the stuff of life here. This is where science and spirituality are tested to their limits, not only for interest's sake but for capitalist reasons. Humanoid machines are being mass-produced in the economy and everyone will eventually own one, live with one or even date one – so this is where humanity is really at the apex of its search for identity. Having said that, let's look at how scientists and philosophers use these words differently and what they could actually mean.

Conscious
Standard definition: Refers to being awake, aware and able to think and perceive one's surroundings, thoughts, experiences and sensations. A higher level of being conscious allows for introspection, self-reflection and the ability to understand one's own mental state.

Consciousness
A scientist's take: The state of being aware of and responsive to one's surroundings. (This is similar to the definition of the word *conscious* above; there is no real difference in meaning.)

A philosopher's take: Consciousness is basically everything; it is life itself. It is the spaciousness out of which the universe and all its contents are created, including stars, planets and humans. You are materialized consciousness, but there is a part of you that exists and is also not materialized and connected to the whole. This immaterialized part of you is the awareness that lives beyond the body and the mind. From this space you are aware of yourself as a body, but also aware of yourself as part of everything that is not the body.

So can a machine be conscious or gain consciousness? Based on both the scientific and philosophical explorations above, the answer is still no. Machines are not 'awake'; they are merely switched on. They do not perceive through multiple senses; they only observe their external environment and offer logical responses. Machines do not 'experience reality'; they simply exist and interact with the world. Machines do not introspect for emotional growth; they merely learn from their data to offer better solutions. So by all accounts from the outside, a machine can behave exactly like a human but never 'be alive' like one. That is because humans do not only have the capacities 'to perform tasks' or 'get things done' but can also better connect with other humans, explore the nature of existence and evolve into something more, something higher.

SO WHAT IS EVOLUTION THEN?

Whether you've studied Darwinism or not, everyone intuitively knows that humans are always evolving. What this means in simple terms is that humans are getting better and better over time – but at what and to what end?

For the most part we've mainly focused on biological evolution.

We measure this by how the shapes of our bodies and brains have changed over the millennia. We talk about our evolution mainly in mammalian terms, such as how we developed the capacity to walk or talk or make tools and reason. We also look at this topic based on how different we are from the rest of the animal kingdom, why we are superior and how the best of us have survived to keep the human story going.

But what about spiritual or emotional evolution – why do these ideas never enter our global conversation? It would seem that this is the case because we function like a very primitive species. Emotional intelligence, as far as it has been studied, is mainly about how we can manage conflict at work. Its purpose in mainstream culture is reduced to transactional reasons. And spiritual practice is about how much more productive we can be after a quick meditation, or how quickly we can 'manifest our desires'. But whether true or not, these are also the mainstream ideas that reduce spiritual practice to a transactional affair. There is very little conversation about how humans actually get better from an emotional and spiritual perspective, what that means and why that matters. We don't discuss this in the same way as we look at biological evolution, maybe because we think our only reason for being is to survive, and nothing further. So let's explore this a little bit more.

Emotional evolution is about human advancement in areas such as developing self-awareness, transcending codependency, relinquishing anger, overcoming abuse and managing wellbeing. Over the decades we learn more about who we are and we get better at understanding and managing our internal worlds so that we can have more loving and joyful relationships – which is a great metric for evolution in humans. Moreover, emotional evolution is also about understanding what it's like to live in a society that centres on compassion, kindness and equanimity. Over the years we have definitely become more cognizant of this, which is why slavery has been outlawed (although forced labour persists in some places), everyday working conditions have radically improved, households are more functional and racism is starting to lose its grip.

But spiritual evolution is also connected to this. While monks and yogis spend most of their days meditating to reach 'higher states', they also spend a lot of their lives doing two other practical things: using their skills to help the poor and reflecting on age-old scriptures to learn how to live in harmony with nature and society. That's why famous yogis and monks such as Sadhguru and the Dalai Lama use their influence to teach the world what it actually means to live with more compassion and kindness and love towards fellow human beings. Every human values these ideas, but understanding how they are applied is what we are here to learn, and each century we get better and better at actually living these values. Each century we become more willing to live like a unified global community, and this is yet another great metric for human evolution.

So why is this important to know? Well, if we were a more organized global society then we would use these ideas as metrics for human progress. Growing GDP and making sure that everyone has a meal to eat are good goals too. But how our wealth is distributed and the degree to which we help others is largely influenced by our emotional and spiritual evolution. In fact, a lack of emotional and spiritual intelligence is why we live in a world where there are currently enough resources for everyone – housing, food, land and healthcare – but an improper distribution of them. This is because our fears are irrational, our perceptions of reality are skewed and our greed is uncontained. It also doesn't help that we only see our own spouse and children as our family; it only makes biological sense that we care for them more than we would for others because we live with them or produced them. But if we think like this, then we're merely like a pack of lions in the jungle

– nothing more. So what the great philosophers push us to question is whether we are actually more than just our instinct to survive or whether we may be more connected to each other, to other humans on the planet, than we think we are. The great thinkers encourage us to think about our evolution in larger terms.

So where do machines fit into all of this? If our purpose is to evolve in these vaster ways, then machines are here to make this possible. AI is here to take care of the grunt work so we can focus on higher-order needs that require a great deal more intention and contemplation. Rather than worry about how AI will get smarter than us, which it will in many ways, maybe this is how AI is helping us to evolve, by encouraging us to think about what makes us different, but also by pushing us towards deeper reflection about our existence, our values and our reasons for being.

Eckhart Tolle questions this beautifully when he asks, 'Is more information going to save the world, or faster computers, more scientific or intellectual analysis? Is it not wisdom that humanity needs most at this time?' He then says that wisdom is to be found in silence and silence is intelligence itself – that is where we find answers to our problems. This 'silence' is that which is often available to you when you sit in meditation, take a long walk into nature, or just stop and daydream into the abyss. But these are not his ideas: they have been echoed for decades by other greats such as Einstein, Krishnamurti and Henry David Thoreau. For centuries, these deeper capacities have been available to us, but now, with machines on the rise, they will become a critical source of direction for developing future societies.

INTUITING THE BEST FUTURE
Periods of silence and contemplation give us access to intuition, and intuition can be defined as *knowing without evidence.* Many

great scientists have known to feel that something is true by means of hypothesizing. They can't explain how they know it is true, or how it makes sense; they simply 'know it' and then attempt to use the tools of science to prove it. Some philosophers say that this is knowing something in your soul. For all we know, the idea could have just landed in your head, but even so, it had to come from somewhere beyond you, if it is not connected to the data within you.

Even so, it is safe to say that machines can create new ideas from old ideas – pattern recognition and new iterations of patterns based on mixing existing ingredients in new ways. But they cannot conceive from a higher, more mystical or ethereal place. So if society has depended on us having hunches or hypotheses to progress into what it is today, then it would seem that we will continue to need access to this 'senseless' place. The future of society is still largely dependent on humans. A prosperous society is still largely dependent on our capacity to conceive in this unique way and create.

Sometimes humans need to take illogical paths to get to higher or better places. When you observe the actions of many brilliant CEOs, it is easy to doubt them in the early stages. Their actions just don't make sense. But they and their immediate team members just know that they are headed in the right direction. And after much criticism they eventually arrive where they said they would or somewhere even better. We've all seen this with Elon Musk, Steve Jobs and Kanye West. Could a machine do that? No. A machine is built to follow logical protocol and not make illogical decisions. It could study human behaviour and case studies to learn how to make big bets on illogical paths. But this is where human and machine differ. At some point, when things are super illogical, these CEOs use their gut, their intuition, their instinct. There is something more mammalian or mystical at play here, and machines just don't have access to that.

Creating a better future for humanity is also not only about creating solutions that are oriented to return on investment (ROI). Yes, you can program a machine to consider other variables, such as climate emissions, fair trade and ethical practice, but how do you program it to create in humanity's best interest, or society's best interest? That is a harder question. Those of us who intend to do the best for humanity are often guided by decisions that don't look good in the short term but otherwise benefit us in the long run – this is yet another intuitive decision. Sometimes human evolution looks like taking one step back before taking two steps forward.

Robots could also be programmed to create futures that consider humanity's best values, but how and in which context those values are interpreted is totally case by case. What seems like a good values-driven decision in context A may be a bad values-driven decision in context B – and this isn't based on preconceived rules but rather on our 'feeling' of what is best to do at a certain time. It seems then that there is no perfect version of humanity: we are always in a continuum of becoming. Some would say this is a weakness of humans versus robots; others would say this is the perfection of the collective human soul – knowing how to do the right thing, at the right time.

MENTAL MODELS

- **What is a soul?** It is the *life force* that exists beyond your mind and your body. When the brain is dead and the mind cannot function, then what sits on the operating table is more than a body. You know this; that's why you won't just switch the oxygen machine off. That 'life' or *life force* that you consider keeping alive is another word for awareness or soul. But machines do not have souls; they are merely electronics that are switched either on or off.

- **Evolution in a nutshell**: Biological evolution is one type of human feat, but we must also consider emotional and spiritual evolution. Biological evolution is about how you survive among the best; spiritual evolution is about how you harmoniously coexist with all. For an intelligent species, the latter is a better measure of human success.

- **Meditation is our superpower**: Meditation may prove to be more than just a relaxation tool; rather, it is a tool for tapping into vaster inspirations and developing more creative solutions. While there is much to still figure out about what the difference is between humans and machines, what we know for sure is that robots cannot meditate – that is our primary superpower, which robots can never imitate.

THE ROLE
OF EMOTIONS

There is a TV show on Netflix called *La Grande Maison Tokyo*, about an extremely talented Japanese chef who focuses on creating the very best French cuisine that he hopes will one day earn him three Michelin stars. The show explores the trials, tribulations and emotional hurdles of assembling a great team, restaurant and menu to achieve this ambitious goal.

In one scene, a waitress gets caught in her attempt to poison a dish and thereby sabotage the restaurant. It is unclear what her motivation was, but after seeing the restaurant staff work so tirelessly towards their goal for many episodes, it is hard for the viewer not to feel immediate anger towards the waitress. At this point, it seems appropriate that the kitchen will now reprimand her and immediately fire her for this unthinkable act.

But what happens next is fascinating. First, right after she is confronted, she is given the chance to explain herself. And then, before letting her leave, she is offered a meal. While she is eating it, it becomes clear that the restaurant owner unknowingly damaged her father's reputation several years earlier and that this was her attempt at revenge. Moreover, after explaining herself, the entire restaurant staff assesses that her actions were completely reasonable and logical – and so the owner rehires her on the spot. She is a world-class sommelier and they need her to earn the three stars; she has expressed her anger and shown remorse, and in that moment it seems obvious that all humans make mistakes, often responding irrationally to long-held emotional pain. So, in this context, rehiring her is a completely logical course of action.

But in the heat of the moment, would most humans naturally reach the same mature and intelligent conclusion? Probably not. Emotions often hijack our higher-reasoning abilities, and so it is evident that machines can probably make much better decisions for us in many situations where emotions could lead to poor decisions. So, while it may not make sense for a bunch of robots to run a kitchen, it is precisely this line of thought that pushes scientists to question where humans fall short or where robots may be better placed to achieve higher returns. This should then make us question what our emotions are for, where they are needed and how they differentiate us from machines in ways that give us a place in future societies.

SO WHAT IS AN EMOTION?

Emotion is literally *energy in motion*. Moreover, your body simply responds to the way you think, feel and act. When you are happy, you release happy hormones such as serotonin, which can make you feel 'high'. And when you are depressed, you can cause fluctuations in oestrogen, which can make you feel 'low'. In other words, emotions can also be defined as *your body's reaction to your mind.*

That said, it's worth exploring what our emotions are. Psychologist Paul Ekman, whose research is often referenced, said that there are six core emotions that are universal across all peoples: fear, disgust, anger, surprise, joy and sadness. Later, another psychologist, Robert Plutchik, introduced a new idea called the wheel of emotions, which is used in schools to help children learn about their feelings. It retains some of Ekman's original core emotions but includes at least 24 others. This was probably when research started to show that we have a wide range of emotions that can be experienced to different degrees. In Plutchik's research, for example, we find that anger isn't the same in everyone and that it can be felt at different intensities: for some it can be experienced as rage, while for others it can be experienced as mild irritation or annoyance. One type of anger may require a very different response from another, so this was useful to help people deal better with the core emotions.

From the Buddhist perspective we only have two core emotions: fear and love, from which all other emotions stem. All pleasant emotions – such as joy, happiness, excitement, optimism, satisfaction, hope and peace – stem from love. And all unpleasant emotions – such as envy, contempt, shame, guilt and anger – stem from fear. Also according to the Buddhist perspective, some of what we consider positive emotions are not strictly emotions but rather states of being and therefore part of our true nature: love, joy and being.

But in psychologist Plutchik's perspective above, some of the emotions stemming from fear are far more intense than others, which indicates a further distance from your true nature. For example, despondency, which is what people feel when they lose all hope in life, is much further away from joy than anger or guilt. By contrast, pleasant emotions such as satisfaction are also much further from joy than excitement and enthusiasm. Of course we're not supposed to be enthusiastic all the time, but too much time spent in anger or guilt, as many humans live today, is also an indication of a life poorly lived – and of the need to make bolder decisions that better serve your reality. Sometimes, however, someone may have lived in a terrible situation for so long that they think their life is bad when it is actually good. If you are in such a position, and you are angry, then it is time to change your situation internally – to change your thoughts and see the world with fresh eyes once again.

WHAT ARE EMOTIONS FOR?

Harvard psychologist Susan David has a simple explanation for the purpose of emotions, saying that they are mere data points that help us understand ourselves and make decisions. This makes sense if *emotions are the body's reaction to the mind*, because that would mean that emotions are just thoughts literally felt in our biology. They are there to give us clues about what to do and when to do it. Sometimes they are felt like a passing wind, the same way you feel sad in an emotional movie or when you feel joy after hearing a joke, but at other times they are actionable information.

Also, while some emotions develop over time to help us cope with our external environments, others are more hardwired or simply come with the 'package'. This doesn't mean that they are always switched on; it simply means that they are available for activation when stimulated or needed for a specific reason, such as the following:

- **Survival**: We've evolved to survive, and some emotions are designed to help us do so. You see a lion and think 'dangerous animal'. Then that thought triggers fear, and fear turns into cortisol, which enables your muscles to move into flight mode so you can get out of harm's way.

- **Growth:** You might intellectually know that you've maximized your personal growth in a particular job, but you have to eventually take action on that insight. This may require a depressive episode or chronic anxiety to force you onwards to better pastures. Wharton professor Adam Grant says that an emotion such as anger is probing us to take serious action; it indicates that a boundary has been crossed and that it is time to move on. So if this emotion is growing at work, then you are literally being pushed to make the required changes.

- **Connection:** You may come to the same workplace every day with the same people, simply to achieve the same robotic business goals, but it is the emotions you feel around them and that they feel around you that help you all connect on more levels than work itself. Emotional cues help you talk at lunch, connect socially in the evenings or get together romantically in the long run.

- **Support:** Some people struggle in their internal worlds; they have unresolved emotions and mental health challenges that prevent them from living a great life – and the way they behave often indicates these emotions. We all feel each other's emotions too, and this prompts us to help our fellow humans so we can all progress together. Few things feel as good as being heard, and millions of people could use just five minutes of that to make it through the day or to make a big new decision in their lives.

- **Transactions:** Many big industries, including insurance, banking and consulting, are already largely run by computers. Around 80% of the value your banker provides to you is already produced by a computer that analyses your accounts, reads market movements and applies automated risk models – all while providing recommendations on what to do next. So why should your banker be paid for a full-time job?

Because he (or she) is always available for your emotional needs. He is there to provide context, perspective and reassurance, so you can *feel like* your cash is in good hands. So, while you are definitely getting good financial advice, you are also effectively buying human connection.

This is perhaps the best part about AI: it will make clear what value we actually provide or what really moves us as humans, so we can double down on that. Emotions can prove to get in the way of good decisions, but sometimes emotions enable decisions, without which markets cannot and will not function. This is also largely why the phrase 'it's not what you know, it's who you know' is, for better or for worse, the nucleus of economic activity.

CAN COMPUTERS HAVE EMOTIONS?

If emotions are merely data points with a predictable set of decision paths, then a computer can easily organize this data and appear to be emotionally intelligent. This is probably why there is a massive movement towards chatbot dating in Japan. A lot of young people are finding comfort in being understood by robots in ways that they have not yet experienced with other humans. So, just as we use the data of our emotions to make sense of our inner and outer worlds and to make decisions, a computer can also use the data of all human emotions to help people understand and respond to the world around them.

Machines can also, with much better accuracy, read human tone and facial expressions to determine the emotions being felt. So if there are inconsistencies between what a person is saying and how they are saying it, a computer can pick this up much faster than a human can, without the 'feeling of internal doubt'. The only thing a computer cannot do is intuitively elicit when everything seems logical at the surface but otherwise just 'doesn't feel right'. That is still key to successful relationships and strategies.

So could computers that have advanced emotional intelligence still replace us in some ways? Yes and no. ChatGPT is proving to be super useful in supporting people with basic mental health challenges. And considering that so much of the data and research that is used to train actual human psychologists is now fed into ChatGPT and other AI tools, it is obvious that a computer can make all the psychological conclusions that a well-trained human can. Of course, being *well trained* isn't everything. Just because you studied all the books doesn't mean you're a great therapist. You need to learn to connect with your patient, be present with them, listen actively and hypothesize where theory alone isn't enough. These are all good indicators of a great therapist and part of the reasons why someone would choose a human over a robot.

But as we see in the movie *Her*, Scarlett Johansson's voice can be pretty reassuring – and wonderfully attractive – and with all the cutting-edge scientific research just sitting at the tip of her silicon brain, it's not hard to imagine that many will find great support from a robot in therapy too. So people might augment their in-person therapy with AI therapy; it's what people do now in one form or the other anyway. People still read books, research their mental health patterns on Google and do their own journalling – all while seeing a therapist once a week. It's just that now all the manual research and journalling will simply become a long recorded conversation with an AI chatbot that will know everything about you, all the time, from every conceivable perspective. Scary and amazing!

However, humans primarily want to connect with other humans – that is a large reason for our existence. It makes us feel happy, united and less alone. So in all situations where a robot can do a job, if the goal is to connect with others, then robots are irrelevant. Even though there are apps we can use to meditate, we still want to attend live sessions just to sit with others. Even though we can take a yoga class on YouTube, we still want to be in a real wooden-floor studio to feel in community with others. Even when everything we want to achieve can be perfectly delivered by a machine, we will still want to see, touch and feel other organic beings. It's more than just a preference – it releases good emotions, essential hormones and keeps us alive.

THE RISE OF THE EMOTIONAL ECONOMY

Now more than ever, people need help with emotional matters. As technology advances, humans are also in a major physiological decline. It's as if things are getting better and worse at the same time. But interestingly these things are happening in complementary opposites. We have been so focused on our outer worlds – building tools, business models and societies – that we have neglected our inner worlds. And this comes not only at a cost to our personal growth: it's costing our economies billions and at the same time holding us all back from being our best selves. That's why therapy is more than an elusive practice for 'those few who need to see a shrink' – it's now a weekly event for the modern-day citizen, and an industry that is on track for the next trillion dollars.

Why? Because everyone is mentally unwell, our brains are overworked, our attention is being shortened, chronic anxiety threatens our extinction and cancer is the new flu. After 200 000 years of biological improvement and evolution, this is the greatest deterioration of our emotional and physical condition. This also makes it the best time in history to learn more about the human condition, and an exciting time to participate in the next guaranteed trillion-dollar industries: wellbeing, somatic therapy, spiritual community and education – all industries that centre on being human, feeling with other humans and being emotionally connected.

Also, with all the public scepticism that is surfacing around traditional healthcare and pharmaceuticals, billions of people are now ready to explore newer, more holistic avenues of health. So if there is migration from that industry to what has been considered 'alternative healthcare', then you have yet another trillion dollars on its way. The entire world is in evolution, and it's not only a technological evolution: we are changing the way we eat, think, speak, behave and navigate human life. This means there is far more opportunity coming than that which will be taken away by robots – and so much of that will rely on our unique humanity or the value we can offer by simply being able to 'feel our feelings with others'.

Moreover, wherever a human is replaced, some customers will feel like they lost a beautiful connection and others will enjoy the efficiency. The latter will simply move on with the AI revolution, while the former will demand human customer service again and therefore move to companies that continue to supply those needs. Economies are always driven by demand, and there will always be people who demand connection with other people.

EMOTIONAL EVOLUTION

What we will soon come to realize is that so much about how we run and do business is based on how we relate to each other versus what we are exchanging with each other, which will also be hugely revealing about how evolved we are as a species. For example, a machine could have all the relevant information it needs to read and respond to your emails for you, but would you want it to? Or is your business as much about managing perceptions as it is about selling products? In other words, if your customers knew everything about you in the same way a machine will need to, could your business still be successful?

What this means is that you sometimes lie or only partially open up to your customers about who you really are, where you really live, how much profit you actually make, or where your suppliers are really based – all because you think you need to 'maintain the relationship' or 'keep the business'. And while a machine could run your business effectively without your involvement, it would need to know all these truths and lies and nuances to run your business effectively. So when we get to this point, it is revealing what kind of a person you are or want to be. It also reveals what emotions, perceptions and values prevent us as a species from holding ourselves to our highest values.

So if we are going to achieve the best tech outcome, then we would need to advance with our tech. Buddhists would say that this means we need to learn how to operate from love not fear. Fear keeps the economic wheel moving but prevents many efficiencies and therefore larger progress. But love, from which honesty, kindness, transparency and openness stem, is actually fundamental to societal progress. And as machines eat up the very last work responsibilities for us, our values and core emotions will be all we're left with. It will also be the time when we will collectively decide what human progress really looks like.

MENTAL MODELS

- **Emotions in a nutshell**: In essence, emotions are just energy in motion and the body's reaction to the mind. But from a functional perspective, emotions are merely data: they help us make sense of our inner worlds and give us clues around how to navigate relationships and life.
- **Can machines have emotions?** No, they cannot feel emotions, as they are not organic beings, but they can read, analyse and make decisions about the emotions they observe in others. They can also mimic emotions with great accuracy by reading your facial expressions and tone.
- **So how are emotions beneficial to humans?** Humans use emotions to connect with each other for transactional reasons, to enjoy each other's company and to grow as people. So if humans use a service primarily for the purpose of connecting with other humans, then whether robots can replace service providers or not is irrelevant.

HOW THE BRAIN WORKS

Lex Fridman, an MIT researcher who also hosts a famous podcast under his own name, regularly has Elon Musk on his show to discuss what's really unfolding in AI. In one episode there was a conversation about Musk's brain chip company called Neuralink, which is controversial to some degree, considering that people are now putting chips into their brains that can help a quadriplegic person walk again but could also be used to hack their brain. But, as Musk put it simply, our brains are already being hacked: the computer started in your lap, then it moved into your hand, and soon it will be on your face and then eventually inside your skull. Babies are already born swiping their fingers at things before ever having interacted with a device; this is called epigenetics, and our hands and necks are already taking on new shapes from too much time spent on our devices. What this means is that in many ways our biology is already interspersed with our technology and, as Musk puts it, computers are already an extension of our brains, whether in our hands or inside our skulls. In other words, just because it seems ludicrous to put a computer inside your brain, it doesn't mean that the computer isn't already 'inside' your brain.

Musk goes on further to describe the structure of the brain when he reminds us that in simple terms it can be divided into two parts: the limbic system and the cortex. The limbic system drives your animal impulses, such as the search for food, sex and power. It basically functions on pure instinct. The cortex, by contrast, enables your capacity to reason, imagine and problem-solve. It is basically your mini computer. So in the future we might consider AI or advanced computers to become the third part of our brains, which may enable us to process at super speed, for example, to solve big maths problems in our heads or learn a language in ten minutes. It's still unclear what this will look like or how it will work or to what degree this is even necessary. But rather than thinking about AI as being this thing happening outside of us, and therefore getting better than us, we ought to think of it as an extension of us: the limbic system + cortex + AI – whether inside of our skulls or not. This would be a more progressive view of the purpose of AI and its place in our future.

HOW DOES THE BRAIN WORK?

Let's start by looking at how the brain is structured. This is what massive teams of software engineers, biologists and neuroscientists need to understand deeply in order to create artificial brains that ultimately support artificial intelligence. The brain consists of three main regions called the cerebrum, cerebellum and brainstem. The latter two are involved with breathing, heart rate and motor neuron skills, which are mainly human needs and therefore barely relevant for robots, so what AI engineers need to really understand most is the cerebrum, which includes:

- **The cortex**: This plays a key role in acquiring, processing, storing and using information. It facilitates perception, memory, attention, reasoning, problem solving and decision making. It is where most of the brain's complex thought processes occur.
- **The limbic system**: This is responsible for emotion, motivation and long-term memory. It controls many of your emotional responses, such as happiness, sadness, fear, anger and pleasure. It plays a big role in how you feel, remember things and respond to the world around you.

Here is an example of how all these functions seamlessly come together:

- **Step 1 – perception**: Sensory information from the outside world is processed by the brain, allowing us to perceive our environment.
  - For example: Let's assume you study plants and one day you notice a pink-coloured tree and try to understand it. Your eyes pick up this visual cue, which then sends a message or image to your brain to begin a problem-solving process.
- **Step 2 – memory and learning**: The brain then stores experiences and knowledge in various regions, allowing us to learn and remember.
  - The images of the pink tree will connect to other parts of the brain where there is prior knowledge about trees. Then it processes and organizes that information among other brain cells related to trees.
- **Step 3 – decision making**: The brain integrates information from the senses, memory and emotions to make decisions.
  - Next time you might see a blue tree and immediately recall all the information about the pink tree and other

trees to study this new blue tree. Your brain is now creating patterns between the pieces of information so you can solve the problem that you first came across.

- **Step 4 – motor control**: The motor cortex sends signals to muscles, allowing us to move.
  - Once you've guessed that the tree colour has something to do with the soil, your brain sends signals to your hand to start digging in the soil around the tree to discover something new or to create new knowledge.

So the brain effectively works as a coordinated system: its different parts interact to achieve different goals. In an organic being this can be very complicated, so computer scientists are primarily focused on modelling the part of the brain where all the calculations happen – the cortex, also known as the mini computer.

HOW DOES AI RELATE TO THE BRAIN?

AI scientists essentially figured out that if they can understand how the cortex works, then they can recreate it with computer hardware and software. And if they can recreate it with computers, then they can create a supercomputer, which is effectively what AI is – a super cortex for very powerful computing. Moreover, what makes this so interesting is that humans can only process 40 bits of data per second, whereas supercomputers can process one billion bits of data per second, making the possibilities for the future infinite if we could accurately model the human brain.

To do that, we needed to understand not only how the cortex works but how it is structured at its most fundamental level. This is easy, because the brain, like all organs, can basically be broken down into cells, and the brain is made up of billions of cells called neurons. At a microscopic level these neurons are connected like a network, with neurons connecting to each other in all kinds of shapes and patterns, unique to each human. Hence the term 'neural network'. Scientists figured that all they needed to do is understand how these biological networks are structured to create artificial networks, upon which they would then replicate and eventually transcend human intelligence. Here's how it works:

- **Neurons**: These cells are like messengers in the brain. Each neuron is connected to many other neurons along bridges called synapses, forming a complex network.
- **Synapses**: When neurons connect and communicate through synapses, they create patterns of activity. These patterns represent different memories, thoughts or pieces of knowledge.
- **Learning and memory**: When you learn something new, your brain strengthens or creates new connections between neurons. This process is how information is 'stored' – not in a single neuron, but in the way groups of neurons are wired together.

The architecture of the brain's neural network looks a bit like a tangled web or mesh, with millions of neurons forming connections with thousands of others to form patterns based on the tasks and information processed. That is why everyone's brain is unique. People who learn more than others form more complex neural connections, creating rich webs of knowledge they can draw from. People's mental webs also look very different based on how or where they accessed this knowledge, which is why you might get five different explanations if you ask five different people to describe a lion in their own words. Objectively it's just the same animal to everyone, but how much each person knows or how they came to learn about lions or their emotional relationship to this topic will all influence how the information is stored.

In short, if the most intelligent humans can only reasonably read one book a week – for example, someone like Bill Gates, who often posts his review of 12 books each quarter – then they can never compete with a computer that can read one book a minute and thereby have infinitely more neural connections than the smartest humans ever can. So you can already see that if a computer also has this 'mental web' of knowledge, and the ability to learn and reason by itself, then its possibilities are unlimited.

WHEN MACHINE BRAINS BECOME LIKE HUMAN BRAINS

Sam Altman, CEO of OpenAI/ChatGPT, wrote a blog post five years after the organization started, to reflect on his journey. To summarize the success of his work in three words he said, 'Deep learning worked.' In other words, his team figured out how to help computers learn just like humans, and that meant they were on track to create a perfect artificial brain.

So what did he mean exactly? Well, computers have always just taken instructions from humans. A human will program an algorithm or formula into a computer to tell it what to do when users click buttons. An engineer tells a computer to give you the answer to a maths problem when you use the calculator on your iPhone. The engineer inputs basic maths rules such as $1 + 1 = 2$ and then the computer learns how to add any size of numbers together. It also does this much faster than humans ever could. This means that computers can 'think faster' than us – and that is already amazing. But what if computers could also 'learn faster than us'? What if computers could teach themselves new languages (as happened at Meta in 2017 when Mark Zuckerberg decided to shut down their new self-learning AI), or ask new questions that humans have never asked, or see patterns in data and make recommendations, or read all the world's information and create new insights, pieces of art or strategies. Wouldn't that be phenomenal? Ultimately a large part of our creativity just comes from reorganizing information that is already out there in different ways. So if a computer has 'all the information out there', then it could also be creative. Sometimes creativity comes from your intuition or 'the gods' but other times it's just about seeing patterns in the world and being the first to package and sell them. That is why ChatGPT is so successful: it has become this computer that can take all the world's knowledge and find new patterns in there to give you the creative answers you want. Moreover, this can be achieved in seconds. Ideas that might have taken you weeks to piece together can now be sourced, organized and packaged faster than ever. And that is an incredible feat.

Hence, the new era of computing is the era in which machines evolve from just thinking faster to learning faster – and that's what is changing everything. That's what deep learning is really about, it's fundamentally what AI is really about, and why Tesla, Oracle and Microsoft are spending in excess of $100 billion to make computers that can learn incredibly well and may perhaps later even act on our behalf. This means that the evolution of computing would be thinking, learning and acting. Once we get to 'acting', we are effectively saying that we trust how well a computer thinks and learns, so we may as well let the computer act on what it knows without our intervention. This is where customer service chatbots have evolved to already, and where Sam Altman and his team believe there is an equally viable path to create the next CEO chatbots that will run billion-dollar companies with no help from humans. That is effectively Silicon Valley's interpretation of AGI, or when computers will be considered to be as smart as humans.

HOW HUMAN BRAINS
TRANSCEND MACHINE BRAINS

An incomplete understanding of intelligence will always lead to an incorrect interpretation of AGI. Most people understand intelligence as only the cortex and don't know much about the other intelligences and their role in helping the species evolve. Devoted logicians (people who swear by logic no matter what) in particular, who think everything can be attributed to their brains alone, will soon see that there is more to humans than just copying the brain.

Sir Ken Robinson said in his TED Talk titled 'Do schools kill creativity?' that 'intelligence is not distinct'. All your intelligences are working together in unique ways: emotions, intuitions, intellectual processes and the five human senses all come together to inform new ideas and create new patterns among information – thereby producing new knowledge. Machines can only work with what they have and make that better. They cannot find new 'inspirations' from nature, meditation, emotional connection, therapeutic discovery, taste or smell. All these experiences are often fundamental in channelling new ideas to the brain so that new logic, science and frameworks can be created.

Moreover, machines may be able to reorganize philosophical ideas in ways that surprise humans; so, if you ask ChatGPT an existential question, you may still find an incredibly useful answer. But AI cannot spiritually reflect on how ideas best fit together in any given circumstance. Sometimes real human intelligence involves moral reasoning, empathy and ethical decision making in complex, ambiguous situations – often where there are no clear answers. In high-stakes situations, these types of decisions are made case by case, through a thread of discussions by groups of people attempting to arrive at outcomes that both 'look' right and 'feel' right. This happens every day in tough business decisions, policymaking, law, corporate governance, and even manufacturing or distribution. Sometimes the choices or decisions we make are so illogical that it's hard to think that a computer, which is purely logical, could also help us arrive at those same great conclusions.

Still, the future is not about human versus machine. If it typically took 12 months for 50 people in government to make a policy decision, AI may reduce that time to 12 weeks. AI speeds up the basic phase during which we would typically get tired, mentally bogged down, hungry, sick, busy with kids, or caught up in our traumas and all the other dilemmas that slow down our mental processing power. Now all we need is one good morning to run a great set of questions through AI and we'll acquire all the basics we need. Now we are not spending months trying to find, organize and package information from which to make a decision. With the right questions and the right AI assistant, everything you need is available to you within minutes, and you can now spend the rest of your time discussing, reflecting and deciding. That is what humans are for.

MENTAL MODELS

- **The brain in a nutshell**: Advanced AI is modelled on the brain, which consists of two parts: the limbic system and the cortex. The cortex is your mini computer, where processes such as learning, reasoning, problem solving and creativity occur. AI scientists believe that if they can replicate the functions of the cortex, they can achieve AGI.
- **AI is made possible by three things**: Super-fast computer chips, all the world's data and a leap in programming called deep learning. Computers used to be given rigid instructions; now they are programmed to learn on their

own. The fact that computers can learn so incredibly well is considered revolutionary in computing and forms the basis on which AI promises such a great future.

- **How humans coexist with AI**: AI is not about replacing humans, it's about augmenting them. In some situations humans will definitely be replaced. That is part of how a revolution occurs. But in the long term there is more gain than loss. AI helps humans with the basics (researching, organizing and packaging) and humans get to do what they do best (discussing, reflecting and deciding).

PART 2
ECONOMY

The whole world is just one giant business and it's always been this way. But this is the first time in history where that story might change; it's potentially the last time in history where money is at the centre of our existence.

EVOLUTION OF
AI AS A TOOL

'In my little group chat with my tech CEO friends, there's this betting pool for the first year that there is a one-person billion-dollar company, which would have been unimaginable without AI and now will happen,' says Sam Altman, CEO of OpenAI. If the ambitions of AI and its North Star can be summarized in one sentence, it's the words above. But that's maybe a few more years away. In fact, if we look at how Altman has defined his milestones for success towards AGI at OpenAI, they are organized like this:

- Level 1 – chatbots, AI with conversational language
- Level 2 – reasoners, human-level problem solving
- Level 3 – agents, systems that can take action
- Level 4 – innovators, AI that can aid in invention
- Level 5 – organizations, AI that can do the work of an organization.

The first four levels are pretty easy to understand, but level 5 is probably much vaster than meets the eye. We are talking about machines thinking and acting like the most seasoned Fortune 100 executives, and possibly being able to achieve goals as well as they can. The likely scenario might be that a CEO has an assistant AI CEO to put all the required thinking in front of them, like McKinsey's best consultants, and then the CEO simply uses their intuition and perception of market movements and internal people dynamics to execute on the suggested strategies. But of course the unicorn milestone of level 5 is seeing a company achieve a billion dollars of success with just one person at the helm. This will mean that a machine is doing a lot of acting and that the CEO is simply reviewing. That would be the point at which we could see some aspect of the economy being run by machines, hopefully in a way that is not only about maximizing shareholder returns but that also advances the rest of society.

WHAT IS AI IN BASIC TERMS?

So far we have looked at the aspirations for AI, how it relates to and differs from being human, and how it generally works as a technology. But if you are well versed in the basics, you can build your career or company towards your own level 5. While AI is generally the science of making machines that can think like humans, there are different types of AI that make this all come together. First of all, you need to differentiate between two types of AI – narrow AI and general AI.

- Narrow AI (or weak AI) refers to AI systems that are trained to perform specific tasks. These systems excel at performing the tasks they are designed for but cannot think or operate beyond their trained scope. Examples of narrow AI include:
  - **Voice assistants** such as Siri or Alexa, which give you

answers to specific questions and predict what else you might want to know based on past information and patterns. For example, you might say, 'Alexa, please tell me the time?' and they reply, 'Sure, it's 10:30 EST. It's also 17:30 SAST in case you needed to know.' Alexa has learnt that you are usually interested in knowing SAST time on Mondays, when you have a meeting in that time zone.

– **Autonomous vehicles** that navigate based on specific parameters. Cars are given basic instructions, such as, 'Learn all the ways to move through traffic, avoid pedestrians and figure out how to park.' With narrow AI, a car won't just decide one day that it now wants to learn how to beat an arrogant driver at a traffic light if it has not been permitted or instructed to figure this out by a human first.

• General AI (or strong AI) refers to AI tools that can understand, learn and apply intelligence across a wide variety of tasks – in a similar way to human cognitive ability. General AI, or AGI, would be capable of reasoning, problem solving and adapting to new or unfamiliar situations without human intervention. In future, we can expect general AI to:

– **apply deep understanding of the world** or reasoning abilities across most subjects and topics. For example, without prior human knowledge, a computer could figure out how a particular plant, based on its chemical composition, could be manipulated in a certain way to create new medicine or solve a particular illness. It uses its logic and sees new patterns and makes a bold new suggestion or invention; and

– **learn new things in real time** without human intervention. For example, if a robot is under threat from someone and far away from its owner, then it may learn to seek support from elsewhere, such as a police station, because the police station is closer. In other words, it can learn in real time that there is a better solution than the one that it was programmed to follow. This would be as simple as the robot calculating that its human owner is too far away from it at present and so it does an internal Google search on 'what to do if you believe you are in danger' and the result says, 'call a trusted friend, dial 911 or get to the nearest police station'. Then the robot simply chooses the last option and maps its way there.

KEY TYPES OF AI MODELS

Naturally, there are different types of AI models that make it possible for us to move from narrow AI to general AI, and while we will not cover all the types here, there are a few that you should absolutely know about to understand how AI generally will evolve in business management and people operations.

Rule-based AI (expert systems)

- **What it is**: This is like regular programming but more advanced. You give the AI a bunch of rules to follow, and it makes decisions based on those rules. For example, if you're making an AI for medical diagnoses, you might program the machine to consider options such as:
  - If the patient has a fever, consider a cold.
  - If they have a rash, consider allergies.

  In this model the machine can only offer as many suggestions or considerations as have been programmed into it, nothing more. It cannot search for or think of new answers.
- **Example**: Customer service chatbots that follow a set script. Most of the customer service bots that have been slowly replacing major human workforces across India and America

have been largely using rule-based AI. Companies eventually figured out that roughly 80% of questions asked have the same predictable answers – meaning a computer could easily do the bulk of the work for this department. For the 20% of questions that do not have obvious solutions, the computer simply directs the customer to a real human. This turned out to be a cheap solution that provided the best of both simple AI and human cognition.

- **Key feature**: The AI can only do what it's told; it doesn't learn or adapt.

Machine learning (ML)

- **What it is**: This is where AI learns from data. You give it lots of examples, and it figures out patterns on its own without needing rules for everything. Through an activity called reinforcement learning, AI can learn a lot by trial and error. It gets rewards for doing things right and penalties for mistakes, in the same was as a dog learns tricks by being rewarded with treats. It is used in robotics, gaming and self-driving cars.
- **Example**: Self-driving cars learn to drive safely in test conditions where dummy humans are placed on real streets. In this example you might tell the computer, 'Every time you do not hit a pedestrian, you win. Now figure out all the ways you need to win.' Then the computer programs itself to be a world-class self-driving car. Every time it hits a dummy human, it loses. And every time it avoids the dummy human, it wins. The computer learns in very small trial-and-error situations how to swerve the car when a human jumps in its way. It might hit the human the first ten tries, but by the eleventh try it figures out that it needs to reduce speed by 20 km/h and swerve just ten degrees more to the left to optimally miss its target, which

are the things we never actively think about as humans, we just intuitively know or don't know. But eventually the computer will win 99% of the time, and that's when tech companies get their permits to put these cars on roads all over the world.

- **Key feature**: The AI improves by learning from experience.

Deep learning (a type of machine learning)

- **What it is**: Deep learning is a more complex version of machine learning. It uses artificial neural networks (as in the brain) with many layers to learn from vast amounts of data. This is especially suited to tasks such as recognizing speech or images.

- **Example**: This type of AI can recognize faces in photos or understand spoken language (like Siri or Alexa do) or improve self-driving cars even further. So what makes it more complex than basic machine learning? Machine learning works according to a simple rule, such as 'if this happens, then do that'. Deep learning, by contrast, is more like saying, 'if this happens, then do that; but also consider that this other thing might happen'. In basic machine learning, you can only handle one question at a time, and it often needs help from people to make better choices. But in deep learning, the program can keep asking new questions based on the answers it gets, learning more and more by itself. This is what makes it super amazing. So if we go back to the self-driving car example, let's assume that deep learning also needs to be applied to cars to make sure they are extra safe. In basic machine learning we can tell the computer to make sure that it always avoids hitting a pedestrian and then it wins. But driving can be more complicated than just *avoiding a pedestrian at all costs*. You may be in a situation where a car has to avoid hitting another pedestrian but then also avoid hitting another car or driving off a bridge or hitting a light pole that could cause death to even more people. This is where the ethics of AI need to be considered too, for example 'if I can't avoid an accident, then which is the "best" accident to make; or if one human will definitely have to get hurt in this scenario, then which human takes the hit'. Either way, we are now moving beyond the simple statement 'if this happens, then do that' and towards 'if this happens, then do that; but also consider if this other thing might happen'. While designing the ethics of AI in these kinds of life-or-death situations is incredibly difficult and questionable, what is undoubtedly phenomenal is that, where the average human might think of only eight or ten of these 'if this, then that, but also consider this' scenarios, a computer can consider at least a thousand ways of looking at and understanding something, from a thousand different angles. So the opportunities for this in technology, science, research, business and creativity are endless.

- **Key feature**: The AI can learn to understand very complex patterns from huge amounts of data.

Natural language processing (NLP)

- **What it is**: NLP is a branch of AI and a type of machine learning focused on understanding and generating human language.
- **Example**: These are smart chatbots such as ChatGPT or tools such as Google search that understand what you're asking. We will look more at how ChatGPT works in the next subsection in this chapter.
- **Key feature**: The AI is designed to understand words, sentences and context and offer highly tailored responses each time.

LEVELS OF NLP

Level 1 – basics of NLP

We now go back to Sam Altman's five levels of AI progress towards AGI. Here it is worth understanding the thinking behind the way each level is achieved, so you know how your company and role will evolve in the years ahead. Altman said level 1 was about creating great conversational AI, so that meant that his company needed to master NLP. And the way they achieved that was by creating super-powerful NLP engines called LLMs, which stands for large language models. ChatGPT is an example of an LLM that has trained itself by reading large amounts of English-language text, which then allows it to learn patterns such as grammar, relationships between words, and how sentences are structured. ChatGPT effectively reads millions of books, websites and sentences to learn how language works. Then, once it knows enough, it can understand the questions you ask it and give you responses that are specific to your needs. Here's how the technology works:

- **Pattern recognition**: LLMs such as ChatGPT are really good at recognizing patterns in language. When they read a lot of sentences, they notice how certain words often go together. For example, if they see 'The cat is on the', they learn that the next word could be 'mat' or 'roof'. This helps them make predictions about how sentences will end.
- **Context understanding**: ChatGPT then pays attention to the context of a conversation. This means it looks at the words around a question to figure out what the best answer is. If you ask about ice cream, it knows to think about flavours and toppings, not about cars or books. It can come to this conclusion because all the information it is reading on the internet is telling it that when people talk about ice cream, then they usually talk about flavours and toppings too.

- **Using examples**: An LLM also learns from examples. If it sees many sentences that ask, 'Why is the sky blue?' and learns that the answer usually involves the sun and air, it can use that information to answer similar questions in the future. This helps it make sense of new questions.
- **Combining information**: An LLM can also combine bits of information from different places to create a response. For example, if you ask about cats and dogs, it can pull from what it knows about both animals and explain how they are different or similar.

So, in the early stages, while it appeared that ChatGPT was magical, it still did not really 'understand its answers' as much as it was just predicting what should be said next based on what was asked and what it had learnt from the structure of millions of human conversations. Just because it had all the ingredients and could therefore suggest any dish, it didn't mean that the computer understood what food is, how it should taste and why ingredients should be put together in a certain way in the first place. But it was still a great conversational AI, and that meant that it had achieved OpenAI's level 1 milestone.

Level 2 – what it means that ChatGPT can now 'reason'

As AI continuously evolves, computers are learning more about context and getting better at reasoning. More than merely answering your questions, computers are learning about why you are asking a certain question and what else you might want to know related to that question but may have not yet asked. This means computers are learning to predict answers not only to the questions we present them with but what we might present them with four or five questions down the line – and that is when

AI really appears to be genius. This is how ChatGPT improves itself:

- **Improved training**: Earlier versions of ChatGPT were less good at understanding context and making connections between ideas. Over time, as it was trained with more data and better techniques, it has become better at reasoning. This means it can create answers that make more sense and are more thoughtful.

  - Earlier versions of ChatGPT might have struggled to follow specific business conversations. For example, if you asked, 'What's the best marketing strategy for an e-commerce store?' and then followed up with, 'How should we adjust for seasonality?', it might not have connected the two questions. Now, ChatGPT understands that you're talking about the same e-commerce store and provides tailored advice for adjusting marketing strategies based on seasonal trends.

- **Complex questions**: ChatGPT can now handle more complex questions that require some logical thinking. For example, if you ask it why something happens and to explain the reasons, it can do that better than before.

  - Before, if you asked, 'How can we improve employee retention?', it might have given a general answer such as 'offer better benefits'. Now, it can dive deeper into the complexities of the question, suggesting ideas such as improving company culture, offering career development programmes, using employee feedback systems and fostering work–life balance – all based on specific business needs.

- **More natural conversations**: With improved reasoning, ChatGPT can have conversations that feel more natural. It can follow along better, respond appropriately and make connections between different topics, which makes it seem smarter.

- Earlier versions of ChatGPT might have struggled when the conversation jumped between different topics, such as finance and human resources (HR). Now, if you ask, 'What are the best ways to cut costs in operations?' and then switch to 'Also, how can we boost employee morale?', ChatGPT can handle the transition smoothly, providing cost-saving tips and morale-boosting ideas in one coherent discussion.

Of course ChatGPT is recording all the conversations that its 200 million human users are having with it every day right now, and that is how it is learning context and good conversation flow. We are feeding the beast and training it into what it will soon become based on who we are, what we care to know about and how we care to know about it. But this is effectively how ChatGPT evolves from a simple conversational app to a powerful reasoning AI as represented in level 2 of Sam Altman's AI roadmap.

Level 3 – the introduction of AI agents

'GenAI' was always the big word that crowded the room when OpenAI started becoming famous, and that's because the name represented how AI was introduced to us and how we used it. GenAI just stands for generative AI and refers to AI systems such as ChatGPT that are capable of generating content such as text, images or code that are great for tasks such as writing, summarizing and translating. However, GenAI is a technology that just creates; it does not act. In order to act, it must be prompted or instructed. Hence, it does not have agency or take actions on its own.

Agentic AI, by contrast, does have agency and acts independently. It not only creates content but also makes decisions on its own to achieve specific goals. For example, you might have an AI agent connected to your email account. It will read all your emails for you, write responses and then either give you an opportunity to read some of those mails before you send them off or automatically send them on your behalf, based on the permissions you give it. For example, in cases where there is little to no variability, you might let the agent take care of everything for you. You might just tell the AI agent to always read and accept calendar invites from your boss because you always say yes anyway. This frees up your time from having to read those emails, respond and add events to the calendar.

Agentic AI will increasingly make us realize how predictable our work and our lives are. Agents will help us find patterns between things – and that's when we will realize that there are probably just ten types of emails that everyone receives, no matter what they do: calendar invites, presentation decks, meeting notes, strategy thoughts, complaints, customer questions, training requests, HR challenges, or opportunities and memos about future decisions and thinking. That's it. Our working lives are not as complex as we might think. That's why research shows that people who spend 30 minutes meditating every day can often transcend the complexities of their 'monkey minds' to overcome their state of restlessness and just get stuff done. But most people probably take eight hours to get two hours of work done. Not because the work is difficult, but because their minds are unorganized. Most people's thinking is unclear, emotionally burdened and anxiety-ridden. So AI agents come to the rescue and find patterns between information to help you quickly accelerate your day. Even if you have confusing relationships, and different styles and tones of speech based on who you're emailing, or different strategies with different types of clients and colleagues – all of these patterns can be picked up in minutes by an AI agent that has read all your emails and documents from the past five years. All the ducks can be lined up for you every morning to simply tell your agent 'yes, send that email' or 'no, edit that email like this' or 'yes, always automatically reply like this to these types of emails and clients'. Literally life-changing.

Level 4 – innovators, AI that can aid in invention

At level 4 of the AI evolution journey we can expect to see AI inventing new ideas. While an LLM such as ChatGPT currently generates responses based on the patterns it has learnt from human language, it doesn't truly 'create' original ideas in the same way as humans do. Instead, it combines existing ideas in new ways. Its creativity comes from the vastness of its training data and its ability to apply this data in new contexts. Here's how it can appear to offer something original:

- **Combining information in new ways**: ChatGPT can take different pieces of information and blend them together in a variety of ways. So where a human might see a dozen different ways of baking a spinach pie, a computer can see a thousand. They might not all be tasty, but some of them will be original and brilliant. Often what we consider creative is merely a new interpretation of an old thing.
  - **Example**: This is largely why homogenous businesses such as restaurants, which fundamentally all sell the same goods, can appear so different from each other and continue to do so well. There might be ten Italian restaurants in your city, all with the exact same menus, but they all have a slightly different interpretation of that menu to keep you interested in wanting to eventually try them all. It's what keeps you constantly curious about wanting to eat at all the best Italian restaurants, no matter where you are in the world.
- **Pattern recognition and extrapolation**: ChatGPT uses what it has learnt to make a good guess at an answer to a question

that has not been asked before. Even if it hasn't seen that exact situation before, it can connect the dots based on what it already knows from other areas of knowledge.

- **Example**: Suppose you are an executive in the mining industry and you ask 'how to design an office space that boosts creativity', ChatGPT could recognize that in other industries, such as Silicon Valley, creative workspaces often have open layouts, areas for relaxation and bright colours. It might suggest incorporating these design elements into your mining offices, even if this specific combination hasn't been applied in your industry before.

- **Generating multiple possibilities**: If you ask the same question to ten different intelligent people, you'll get ten uniquely insightful answers. In the same way, ChatGPT can also consider different ways to answer one question, except all on its own. Moreover, some of these possibilities may feel new or innovative because they offer a combination of perspectives that no one has thought of before.
  - **Example**: If asked how to approach a new market or type of customer, ChatGPT could generate several different strategies, some of which might seem creative because they combine ideas from unrelated fields or apply unconventional approaches.

Again, this is what LLMs can do already or are exponentially getting better at each day. As we move into the future, we can expect this to take on a whole new level. While we, as humans, can still uniquely perceive novel ideas via our intuition, once ChatGPT can 'create new knowledge', or at least suggest ideas for new bodies of knowledge, then AI will have made a massive technological leap from where it is now. Here's how it would differ from AI today and what it might look like:

- **Autonomous problem solving**: Innovator AI will be able to assess challenges and suggest potential solutions independently.
  - **Example**: This could take the form of an AI agent in your email that not only responds to basic emails, but also proposes strategies based on all the data it has about your company, market trends and the customer or colleague you are pitching to. We will soon be waking up to emails that have attached slide decks, revenue reports and strategy frameworks just waiting for us to approve and hit send.
- **Cross-disciplinary creativity**: This AI will combine knowledge from different fields (for example, biology and engineering) to create innovations that break traditional boundaries.
  - **Example**: In the pharmaceutical industry, instead of researchers trying multiple approaches to discover a new drug, Innovator AI could rapidly analyse thousands of potential chemical compounds, suggest novel combinations and run virtual tests to predict their effectiveness. This would accelerate the invention process far beyond human capabilities. Innovator AI could run simulations to test out its inventions in virtual environments before they're built or implemented, optimizing designs before they reach reality.
- **Exploratory scenarios**: It will experiment and explore different pathways to innovation, much like a human inventor might tinker with different approaches to solve a problem.
  - **Example**: Typically you have *thinkers* and *doers* in organizations, and as you move higher up in the leadership chain, you move more towards being an

essential thinker. This means you are not only considering how to manage your internal environment but also considering your external environment to keep your business afloat. With Innovator AI, a computer could help you manage internal activities, keep an 'eye' on external activities, and continuously cross-calibrate between internal and external activities to ensure that you remain on track as a business, based on what is specifically relevant to you. This means your AI could identify new business opportunities by analysing market trends, consumer behaviour and technological developments – as well as suggest new product ideas, sales channels or investment strategies that fit seamlessly into your business model.

It would seem that at this point we will reach a future where our human superpowers will lie in asking the best questions rather than having the best answers. To make business and product decisions, we are typically merely scanning our external environment, and if a computer can do that better and more efficiently than we can, then we evolve from being creators to reviewers. There will still be a market for handmade graphic design work and for handmade leather goods. But for many creators the value added will be about how far one can imagine rather than how well one can use Adobe. As for managers, the human value added will be less about applying the mind to create a brilliant strategy and more about choosing the right strategy, at the right time.

But there is one more part of this evolution that is interesting: the stage at which computers also ask good questions. An AI agent is effectively set up to continuously ask itself new questions that help it reach its goals. In this case we are left with less need to reflect on basic strategic, operational or engineering questions.

We now move to asking more ethical, moral or human-centred questions. We will become master contextualizers and systems architects. This means that if we are presented with five well-solved puzzles, then it will be about choosing the right puzzle, and seeing how it fits into the greater puzzle of what it means to be human at the time.

As computers solve basic business problems, we will have more opportunities to think like philosophers, which is what the world really needs. If AI can always present me with great sales, marketing, product and operations strategies, then running my company for great ROI will no longer consume me as my primary focus. I should then use AI, and my mind, to recreate those strategies in ways that earn a profit but also help my community; make revenue but also assist the environment; help the company remain competitive but also support local producers; create great customer engagement but also aid in their emotional growth; and keep people happy but also help them evolve spiritually. Can you see that there are way more interesting ways to run businesses than we have the capacity or mental energy for today? So, this will become the focus of human effort in the medium to long term. These will be the new questions and models we will run through ChatGPT to optimize our businesses not merely for profit but for maximum positive impact on society and the humans that inhabit it. Our only limitation will be our curiosity surrounding the pursuit of an insanely great human experience.

Level 5 – AI that can run an organization

As we reach level 5, OpenAI says that the first interpretation of AGI is 'AI that can do the work of an organization'. So, what do they mean by that and how would this work? It's actually pretty simple: it's a company of AI agents that can manage its own business activities as well as create its own agents as it sees new use cases. So, just like a human manager will constantly observe the dynamics of the business and create new processes or tools or make decisions to improve operations, AI will eventually be able to observe an operation and constantly update itself. As long as it knows what its chief goal is – maximize profits or increase revenue and reduce costs – it can figure out everything else from there. You only need to program other rules into it, such as 'don't break the law, ever', 'pay taxes on time' and 'always keep customers and suppliers happy, as long as XYZ ethics are maintained'. Like McKinsey consultants, your AI agents are formulaic and can therefore create and execute on any strategy that pursues its core goal, profitability, with some light consideration of other important variables.

But, of course, what also needs to be considered is that the word *organization* largely refers to the 'organization of people, process and product'. So, while AI can master process and product, in many cases people cannot just simply be replaced or ignored. Organizations typically have entire ecosystems of human suppliers, partners, shareholders, customers, employees, board members and government officials – all with an interest in the business. And so much about being successful is about effectively managing those relationships and friendships. This means that even if machines are capable of running businesses, in some cases it just won't work. Even so, this doesn't mean that some companies won't get this right. There are still industries where people will get together across the supply chain and make it their mission to achieve this goal, and they will. For them, shared relationship goals will evolve from working together *in the business* to working together *on the business* – and letting machines do the rest. This is the future that is already happening right now.

MENTAL MODELS

- **Five levels towards AGI**: Level 1: Chatbots; Level 2: Reasoners; Level 3: Agents; Level 4: Innovators; and Level 5: Organization builders and managers. These five levels represent OpenAI's interpretation of the journey towards AGI.

- **Key types of AI models and programming**: Narrow AI (AI that does specific tasks such as customer service) vs. AGI (AI that does a variety of tasks and can solve anything like a smart human); rule-based AI (AI that merely uses the information it has in the way it is programmed to use it) vs. machine learning (AI that can teach itself new things and offer new ideas); and NLP (a type of AI that learns to understand human language) vs. LLM (the engine that supports NLP – for example, ChatGPT is an LLM that works to understand how humans talk and think).

- **GenAI vs. agentic AI**: GenAI (generative AI) refers to AI systems that are capable of generating content such as text, images or code. But GenAI only creates; it does not act. In order to act, it must be prompted. By contrast, agentic AI acts independently. It not only creates content, but it also makes decisions on its own to achieve specific goals without human intervention.

6

STRATEGICALLY IMPLEMENTING AI

'Discovery is a data-science-heavy insurance company, so becoming an AI-powered company is a natural step for us,' says Derek Wilcocks, CIO of the Discovery Group. 'We rely on our data being well organized because we literally run our entire insurance philosophy on being able to model data correctly. This makes the AI leap easy for us. But most companies will struggle at first. They will most likely have their data all over the place, repeated in some places, or entered incoherently across multiple databases. This means that they will have to clean their data before they can use large language or LLM models and really benefit from AI. What you get out is only as good as what you put in.'

What Wilcocks's words imply is that while the tech is advancing very quickly, the rate at which AI will reach your organization or become a critical feature might look very different. Each company will need to assess where they are at in terms of understanding AI, affording AI and having their data ready for AI. This will determine their journey towards becoming an AI-powered organization.

But let's start with the basics. AI has one main purpose in business, as all business tools do: to maximize profit by cutting costs and increasing revenues, and everything else you need to know will be centred on this. Without getting caught up in all the hype, each organization and its people simply need to apply AI in an experimental way across different functions and see what works and what doesn't in terms of driving profit. New technology is always introduced to us in an aspirational way, mainly because it sells good stories in the media but also because it gives companies such as Apple and Google leverage to sell their hardware and software tools to us, for example the 'all new AI-powered iPhone 16' or 'Google's AI-powered new Gmail'. But while AI will eventually live up to its promises of perfection, each company has to also figure out how to achieve its ROI with new AI tools in its unique context.

Secondly, AI is merely a prediction tool that guesses what should be done based on what it is given. It guesses how to reply to an email, or how to deal with a customer or how to draft a social media post. Over time, AI gets better at achieving the right outcomes for you or predicting the best responses for you. But in the short term, AI models are still in training. As they make mistakes, people need to correct those mistakes – and then AI gets better. For example, when you ask ChatGPT to write a marketing strategy for you, right below the answer it asks you if you want to regenerate the answer. This gives the computer a chance to show you something that is more suited to you. Moreover, 2 000 other people on the planet are probably asking ChatGPT the same question, on the same day, and as they talk to ChatGPT, they keep telling it things that make its answers better, such as 'Okay, great strategy, but please include a tactical plan or include tools I should use or include other social media platforms I should post on'. All these questions, if repeated often enough, tell ChatGPT that these are important factors to include when answering a question such as this one, and that's how it gets better at giving you exactly what you need. But in each business there are unique use cases, patterns, and levels of customer or supplier sensitivity. This means each business has to find out on its journey where AI is making good predictions versus where its predictions need more fixing or human intervention.

Thirdly, while the greater story of AI is about how it will take over our roles, in the short term it is about AI as an augmentation tool rather than a replacement tool. Even if AI agents are doing work, it is still worthwhile having them do the work alongside the people they may or may not eventually replace. Maybe, in some cases, humans will be there to double down on areas that AI cannot get right, no matter how hard it tries, or AI agents will permanently replace some aspects of roles but also create new opportunities within those roles for which humans will be needed. How markets, technology and your specific business model will transform is yet to be seen. Your business will not work like other businesses. But what you know for sure is that you definitely need people and AI in the medium term, and you will very likely need people and AI in the long term.

BUSINESS GOALS WITH AI

Every business has goals – within each department and as an organization as a whole. Whatever those goals are, the only reasonable question in this context is, 'How can AI help me achieve those goals better, faster or more efficiently?' This is what the world's biggest companies are trying to understand as they invest in AI. A simple value chain formula for them might be, 'If I apply AI tools to the W department, then it will help me achieve my goals

X times faster, and it will save Y hours per year, saving the company Z dollars'. For example, if AI replies to all my basic customer queries on my behalf, then I save three hours each day, or 720 hours per year, which means either that the company can save 30 working days a year where they don't bring me into the office and cut my pay, or that they can use those 30 free days to give me some other task that they might have paid a brand-new employee to do. These are the types of formulas companies are chasing, but how they choose to act on the results is a whole separate affair.

Likewise, AI might give companies brand-new goals that they never had before. For example, AI agents could be used to analyse all your company data, customer acquisition trends and market movements to suggest your next business opportunities. It may find new opportunities within the existing business model or suggest entirely new ventures that can leverage your existing customer base and core competencies. Most business leaders and entrepreneurs are so busy managing and growing their existing business that, even while they know that diversifying their investments is important for long-term sustainability, they simply don't have the time and mental capacity to tinker with new ideas. But in this way, a CEO can outsource the diversification strategy to an AI agent and then, when ready, they can task a team to execute on that strategy. Here's a simple list of potential AI goals for your organization:

- **Reduce time**: Automate repetitive tasks to save time and reduce errors, for example in invoicing, data entry and obvious customer queries.
- **Reduce risk**: Analyse large volumes of data to provide better insights and guide more informed decisions, for example a financial analyst could run their models through AI to see if anything was missed.
- **Reduce cost**: Streamlining operations through AI can lower

operational costs by reducing manual labour and minimizing inefficiencies, such as getting AI agents to read 1 000 résumés and quickly book calls with potential great talent.

- **Increase revenue**: Tailor marketing, sales and service interactions to individual customer preferences to increase engagement and loyalty, for example by sending specific sales offers to specific clients based on past purchase data.
- **Increase retention**: Analyse employee engagement and performance data to identify those at risk of leaving. AI can flag employees showing signs of disengagement, such as reduced productivity or frequent absences, and HR can intervene with personalized retention strategies.
- **Increase innovation**: AI can generate new ideas and simulate product concepts. For example, you can use AI to test new travel packages by analysing traveller preferences and predicting how they'll respond before launch.

So, like all business tools and strategies, AI is aimed at helping companies increase their revenue or improve metrics related to revenue, or reduce costs and improve metrics related to costs. The primary focus in a business context will always be, 'Are we getting ROI with this new AI tech that we are investing in?' If the answer is yes, then AI will keep becoming more and more a part of how organizations work.

WHERE CAN AI BE APPLIED ACROSS THE COMPANY?

Renowned multinational business consulting firm McKinsey starts its AI pitch on its website by saying 'our latest research shows that a majority of firms have adopted AI in at least one function'. Further down the site it says, 'We partner with clients to explore what's possible with AI to set an inspiring vision that wins support across the organization.' In other words, 'Hurry up, people are already beginning with AI in small ways, but, also, here is an opportunity to think bigger.' Outside of their pitch, this also gives us clues as to where and how to apply AI in our companies. We can start by thinking as simply as testing AI with one department, getting results, and then investing deeper and wider. Or thinking broadly and creating a trickle-down effect across the whole organization. In the first strategy this might involve automating most tasks in your customer service department using AI agents. In the second strategy this might mean buying every employee, across all departments, a subscription to ChatGPT to get familiar with the tool and use it in their work. The route you eventually take will depend on your goals, resources and appetite for risk.

Each department in your firm will have numerous activities that could be automated or enhanced or assisted by AI, so deciding where to begin will also be a matter of identifying the easiest, lowest-risk, highest-ROI places for implementation within any department or across all departments. The answer may look different for different firms, but the table shown here provides a simple breakdown of the functions in an average firm and shows how AI might be applied to some of the main activities in each to achieve your business goals with AI.

Department	What it does	AI use cases
Finance	Tracks money, plans budgets and handles payments	• **Expense forecasting**: Predicts future costs (saves costs) • **Fraud detection**: Spots suspicious transactions (reduces risk)
Human resources	Hires people, manages teams and helps employees	• **Résumé screening**: Quickly finds the best candidates (saves time) • **Engagement monitoring**: Identifies unhappy employees (increases retention)

Department	What it does	AI use cases
Sales	Sells products and keeps customers	• **Lead prioritization**: Focuses on likely buyers (increases revenue) • **Sales forecasting**: Helps predict future sales (reduces risk)
Marketing	Promotes products to attract customers	• **Personalized ads**: Tailors ads for customers (increases revenue) • **Advertising budget management**: Optimizes marketing spend (saves costs)
Customer service	Helps customers with questions or problems	• **Chatbots**: Answers basic customer questions (saves costs and time) • **Feedback analysis**: Analyses customer reviews (increases retention)
Operations	Manages daily work and supplies	• **Supply forecasting**: Plans stock levels (saves costs) • **Task automation**: Automates repetitive tasks (saves time)
Product design	Creates and improves products	• **Customer feedback**: Uses reviews for improvements (increases innovation) • **Design suggestions**: Suggests new designs (increases innovation)
Compliance	Ensures the company follows laws and regulations	• **Monitoring laws**: Tracks regulation changes (reduces risk) • **Reviewing documents**: Checks contracts for issues (saves time)
Information technology (IT)	Manages technology and keeps systems secure	• **Cybersecurity**: Detects security threats (reduces risk) • **IT helpdesk**: Solves tech problems automatically (saves time)
Procurement	Purchases supplies and manages vendors	• **Vendor evaluation**: Picks the best suppliers (saves costs) • **Contract optimization**: Analyses contracts (saves costs)
Legal	Handles legal matters and risk management	• **Contract review**: Speeds up legal reviews (saves time) • **Risk assessment**: Identifies legal problems (reduces risk)

HOW TO IMPLEMENT AN AI STRATEGY

Regardless of whether you're the CEO or a frontline manager, it will not be obvious to you whether the AI strategy will come down from the top of your organization or upwards from the bottom. In the early stages it will most likely flow in both directions, as managers and employees rush to familiarize themselves with various AI tools. Either way, chief executives and managers across the firm will generally need to think of a few basic steps and variables when developing an AI strategy:

- **Define the problem**: Identify two to three key business areas where AI will have the biggest impact (for example, customer engagement or automating routine work).
- **Pilot projects**: Start small with pilot projects. Select AI tools that can demonstrate quick and measurable results (for example, a customer chatbot).
- **Invest in data**: Ensure that your business is collecting and organizing data effectively. Your chief information officer and chief technology officer play a critical role here; they need to make sure their data is clean before AI is applied.
- **Build or partner for AI talent**: Whether you're using off-the-shelf tools or creating your own LLMs, you'll need people who understand AI. Either learn as a team, hire talent or partner with a consulting firm.
- **Educate teams**: Help your teams understand the basic capabilities of AI and the impact it might have on their work. Demonstrate the impact AI can have on their key performance indicators (KPIs) and give them room to experiment with tools on their own and provide feedback.
- **AI governance**: Establish guidelines for data privacy, security and ethical AI use. This ensures that you are compliant with the law and builds trust with customers.
- **Set measurable goals**: Ensure that any AI initiative has clear

goals and measurable outcomes (for example, time saved, increased sales and reduced turnover) so you can track the success of AI adoption.

If your pilots work well, scale them across other departments. You can also host organization-wide sessions in each department to see what has worked well where, and how ideas from the bottom can influence or improve strategies from above or vice versa.

Also recognize that your employees are in this ambiguous place between helping you craft a brilliant AI strategy that could tremendously help the firm and fearing that it could replace them. You need them to make the tools better, but soon the tools could be so good, based on their continuous inputs, that you might not even need a person in that role anymore. Moreover, hoping that your staff remain unaware of this is a far reach, so create ways for everyone to contribute to the AI revolution but also create space to address fears in the firm or instil optimism in the fact that everyone's roles will evolve. It may turn out that your staff appreciate this and participate in the changes in the hope that things will magically work out in the end. The best-case scenario is that they actively find new ways to redefine their roles in ways that meet the new needs of the organization and drive new profits. Whatever the outcome, it's a major win–win when managers are simply honest with their teams at this time.

WHAT TOOLS TO USE

In the global race to produce AI business and productivity tools, every software company wants to be a player and seller in this game. This means you'll likely end up with more apps, mix-ups and repeat purchases than are necessary as you get started. A sense of what certain types of apps do and where they fit in the organization will make it exponentially easier for you to know where to begin with AI. Here is an overview of the world of tools.

General entry-level tools

You can buy tools off the shelf that help employees get work done better and faster. These might just be GenAI tools that employees can use to experiment with to become familiar with AI.

This could be a simple subscription to an all-purpose generative AI app, such as ChatGPT, Google Gemini or Perplexity AI to help employees in various departments get help with basics such as writing emails, strategy and market research reports. All these apps do the same thing; they just do it differently. And like all products of early competitors in a new industry, you simply buy the one that feels right for you, is the cheapest or connects best with your current suite of tools.

Function-specific tools

Function-specific tools, intended to help employees do one task really well, are also available off the shelf. Naturally ChatGPT and Google Gemini want to be everything to everyone, so companies that focus on AI for specific cases will probably offer the very best tools.

These tools could be in the form of buying access to Salesforce AI or HubSpot powered by AI to accelerate how you manage sales and marketing. Salesforce has mastered client and lead management, so they will likely be best at creating AI tools that streamline customer service and sales.

These could also be creative tools such as video AI or design AI that help folks in the creative department generate ideas faster. While current tools are getting better over time at producing finished products, they are already very good at generating early ideas that make the creative process much faster.

Vertical and horizontal integration tools

There are vertical and horizontal integration tools that are designed to help departments in your company to communicate better with each other or help your firm to communicate better with other firms in its supply or value chain.

- **Horizontal**: These AI apps or agents coordinate work between different departments in one firm. For example, if you have software that tracks stock levels in your food distribution company, then, based on sales movements for that month each year and typical supplier availability in that month each year, AI can automatically order new stock at the right amounts from the best suppliers at the best price. To get this right, you need AI to talk to databases in sales, distribution and purchasing – and you'll use AI here to create a seamless connection between these departments.

- **Vertical**: Assuming you're a book printer, you might use AI to forecast availability of paper and automatically send you updates from each paper supplier, based on their internal numbers and metrics. This lets you forecast how many books you can print within a given timeframe and whether you need to source more paper. It is called vertical because it connects your business upwards towards your suppliers. Where you typically needed to check with your suppliers manually over the phone or forecast on gut instinct, now AI organizes exact numbers from suppliers for you.

Background tools

Background tools are basically applied to things you already do and they help you do them better. They might help you with GenAI tools internally in your company or by organizing information for you in the capacity of agentic AI so you can get things done faster.

- To get started with these tools, many companies simply buy access to Microsoft Copilot or Google Gemini based on what software they were already using in their company to manage tasks such as email, document creation, spreadsheets and meetings. What these tools promise is to apply their LLMs to these existing apps and make them work better. This means they do things such as read your emails and help you write better responses or record your meetings and help you devise the next steps forward.
- Microsoft Copilot also includes access to a corporate and private version of ChatGPT that reads all emails and internal documents to give employees more specific answers related to their questions inside the company.
- ChatGPT is just an LLM, and in the form of Microsoft Copilot, this LLM is limited to the apps you currently use from Microsoft or the questions you put in to generate answers. But there are also other pieces of your company that LLMs could be applied to – and this opens up a whole new market for apps. You can buy separate LLMs to read all your customer queries and to help you better automate customer service, or you can buy LLMs for engineering that help you better fix bugs in your work or write brand-new code for you. As your business naturally advances with AI, you will consider buying and applying LLMs that specifically support certain functions of your business better than others.

THE CASE FOR AN AI ROADMAP AND STRATEGY

To understand how these ideas apply, we will look at a simple example of a business. Let's assume we are looking at a global travel agency. The main service is to help customers plan trips and book flights and hotels. Imagine the business makes $10 million a year and has 100 employees. One day the CEO comes back to the office from an AI conference and says to his staff, 'We need to think about how to apply AI to our business to remain competitive. Let's have a meeting tomorrow to figure out where to begin.' If this meeting happens, then these are the points that might be explored.

Key goals

- **Improve customer experience**: Personalize trips based on preferences, provide real-time communication and offer faster resolutions to inquiries. *Let's use AI to analyse the past 20 years of our travellers' data to find patterns among customers, and let's make them tailored offers and discount packages.*
- **Automate operations**: Reduce time-consuming tasks such as invoicing, vendor coordination and schedule management. *Let's see if we can automate booking and management of flights, hotels and airport shuttles.*
- **Optimize sales and marketing**: Use data to predict customer behaviour, tailor promotions and increase bookings. *Let's apply AI to our customer data to find out who flies the most in low season so we can market to them in a more tailored way in future.*
- **Enhance employee productivity**: Equip employees with AI tools that help them focus on high-value work instead of repetitive tasks. *If AI can book and manage flights and schedules and answer basic customer queries, then let's spend time building customer relationships with our high spenders and luxury travellers.*
- **Drive innovation**: Explore new travel offerings such as AI-powered virtual tours or augmented reality or AR-based pre-trip experiences. *If we can get clients to experience new*

destinations beforehand in some innovative way, then maybe this will increase bookings.

AI tools to use and areas to focus on

- **Customer service chatbots**: Use AI bots to answer potential traveller inquiries 24/7. For example, a chatbot can manage common questions such as tour dates, payment issues or visa requirements.
- **Marketing analytics**: Implement predictive AI tools (for example, HubSpot AI) to analyse booking patterns and suggest ideal times for promotions.
- **Scheduling and planning**: Use AI for demand forecasting to manage seasonal tour schedules. AI tools from Google can optimize itineraries based on weather or health issues such as Covid-19 or flight price changes.
- **Operations automation**: Automate tasks such as invoicing or expense tracking using Salesforce Einstein or other Software as a Service (SaaS) platforms.

How much to spend on AI

A good benchmark is to start by allocating 5% to 10% of your technology budget to AI initiatives and increasing this gradually as you see returns. For your business's size, an initial investment of $50 000 to $100 000 might allow you to access key SaaS tools such as chatbots and marketing AI. You probably don't need to build custom AI solutions at all – you can use off-the-shelf tools to ensure you control costs while piloting projects. AI investments must show measurable impact. So you will focus on metrics such as:

- customer satisfaction (faster response times via chatbots)
- employee productivity (time saved by automating emails)
- increased bookings and revenue (high-engagement marketing campaigns)

• cost savings (reduced manual labour with automated invoicing).

Let's set short-term ROI goals (3–6 months) for automation projects to track immediate savings, and long-term goals (6–12 months) for customer engagement and revenue growth. For example, if chatbots reduce inbound customer queries by 50%, the cost savings will be evident through fewer support hours needed.

Managing a trip for a client with AI vs. manually

Just so we're clear, let's look at an example of how a trip would be managed with AI compared to how we manage them now. Let's say we are working with our student travel department, where we take students on tours to different countries. This is how our business and process would change.

Traditional process

• The operations team collects information from students and parents over multiple emails and phone calls.
• A tour manager coordinates flight bookings, hotels and transportation manually, often juggling changing schedules.
• Any changes (such as a flight delay or visa delay) require immediate manual communication with all vendors and clients.
• Follow-ups are done through emails or phone calls, creating gaps in service.

AI-powered process

• An AI system collects all necessary information from students and parents via an automated form and chatbot.
• The system suggests optimized travel plans, handling hotel, flight and transport bookings based on historical data.

- If there's a flight delay, the AI sends automatic notifications to buyers and offers rebooking options instantly. Also, if the timeline between getting a visa and going on the trip doesn't fit, then students who have not received visas yet can be automatically informed as early as possible, which will prevent disappointment.
- After the tour, an AI tool sends personalized follow-up emails to parents and collects feedback to improve future trips. This will improve our business tenfold as parents want to be involved in ensuring our trips are good value for their children each year.

Long-term vision and roadmap

Let's consider how we might roll this out. We will set up a pilot project that's really easy. Once that achieves some success, we can move on to investing in more ambitious milestones. This is how we could foresee our process unfolding.

Phase 1 – immediate (0–3 months)
- Pilot AI tools such as chatbots and automated invoicing.
- Train staff on AI tools to ensure smooth adoption.

Phase 2 – short term (3–6 months)
- Expand AI use in marketing and sales with personalized campaigns.
- Automate scheduling and vendor management to improve logistics.

Phase 3 – long term (6–12 months)
- Integrate AI across departments and evaluate impact regularly.
- Explore new AI-driven offerings, such as virtual tours or augmented reality previews.

Pilot project example:
AI-powered customer service

Let's start small with a pilot project in customer service using an AI-powered chatbot. Here's how it could work:

- **Set up**: Deploy a chatbot on our website or WhatsApp to answer traveller queries about bookings, travel requirements and payments.
- **Test**: Monitor its performance for three months – track response times, customer satisfaction scores and how many queries are resolved automatically.
- **Adjust**: Use feedback to improve the bot's capabilities and extend it to handle more complex queries.
- **Scale**: If the pilot succeeds, integrate the bot into email communication or travel apps to provide consistent support across platforms.

TOWARDS A FULLY MACHINE-RUN COMPANY

In the previous chapter we talked about how some companies and value chains will attempt to integrate AI and become fully machine run. While that sounds far in the future, many companies already have the ingredients for this and are close to this reality. South African CEO Kobus du Toit of Workflow Jam, a company using AI to integrate workflows for its clients, said the following:

> The average F500 company uses 2 730 apps to run their business, but only needs 77. So the idea is to find any duplication of activities, goals and conversations so that you can streamline your venture and really see what is happening. Moreover, once you streamline your workflow and reduce your tools to the essentials, you can start to see how to get the tools to talk to each other. This already provides opportunities for creating

AI agents to integrate or execute tasks that humans typically
do manually. Then, once you apply those agents, you will start
to see that your business did not need as many apps, or people,
as you thought it did.

Granted, this extreme case is only relevant to some companies,
mostly software or SaaS companies that offer very specific services
with almost 100% predictability about what the customer will
want each time, without a human ever being present.

For example, an app such as Docusign has been a staple product for almost every CEO on the planet. The app barely changes
over the years and it only does one thing really well – it helps you
sign contracts. As a result, as long as you continue using it for
that goal, you don't really need the app to do anything more, nor
do you ever need to talk to the staff at the company – unless you
want to buy a bulk subscription for your team. So what you have
is a product that was made once, and made well. It requires no
innovation and requires no upgrades. Moreover, as a customer,
I don't even want the product to have any upgrades, because I don't
want any distractions. Like Docusign, there are plenty of apps
that are super successful for just doing one thing well for years,
with millions of users and no interaction between customers and
sellers. So if a few human engineers can get together and create
the perfect app, then they can hand it over to an AI CEO to manage the rest into perpetuity.

A company, for the most part, is not really a complicated affair.
You make something, you sell it, and you coordinate between
making and selling. Another way of looking at this is saying that
a company can just be broken down into three key areas of
responsibility: product, sales and operations. In a software company such as Docusign, where there is little variability – no need
for suppliers; no need for customer relationship building; no

complicated user questions that can't be answered by a chatbot; just one place that can always reliably sell the goods (the app store); an easy refund policy (you don't like it, you cancel and you don't pay); a dead simple advertising strategy that can run on autopilot; no considerable need for software updates; almost predictable engineering bug fixes that can be solved with AI agents; and the possibility of updating its user interface on its own as the Apple App Store updates its policies – you have a company that can effectively run on its own. This is a simplified version of that story, but you can already see that we are not far from this reality, especially in industries where fewer people are needed than others to run multi-million-dollar companies.

MENTAL MODELS

- **Why AI in business**: AI in a business context only has one goal: to increase profits. That means companies will need to find use cases where AI either increases revenue or cuts costs to determine whether AI is a valuable investment or not.
- **AI is always applied to data**: If you are using AI in your company through an app such as Microsoft Copilot or some other LLM, it is always applied to your existing data to give you suggestions. Therefore you need to make sure that your datasets are clean and organized – for example, there should be no duplication of customer names with varying information in different places – so that the AI can give you accurate answers.
- **Where to start with AI**: Many companies start with small-scale pilot projects to get a feel for how AI works and where it will work best for them, based on their needs and budgets. This means you could either buy your team

access to ChatGPT and let them play with it – this would be a purely generative AI experiment – or you can invest in automating one department, for example customer service. This is where most companies begin, because customer service is most predictable for AI – this would be an agentic AI experiment.

7

WHAT WILL FUTURE ECONOMIES LOOK LIKE?

Ethan Mollick, associate professor at the Wharton School of the University of Pennsylvania and author of *Co-Intelligence: Living and Working with AI*, typically writes on social media about AI's impact on the business world. In one of his posts, he mentioned someone who had an insider view of OpenAI and who said, 'the fact that OpenAI is making billions is accidental. Their goal is not to become some great productivity tool in business, it's to achieve AGI.' On their website, OpenAI even states, 'Our mission is to ensure that artificial general intelligence – AI systems that are generally smarter than humans – benefits all of humanity.' Of course, no one at OpenAI is complaining either: the revenue from business subscriptions to OpenAI is paying the bills to get to AGI. From this perspective, well-meaning AI companies with ambitions to change the world for the better probably have the following deployment roadmap from a revenue perspective:

- **Help companies get richer:** If AI can immediately be used to help companies cut costs and increase revenues, then in a world built on capitalism, AI already becomes a very important tool. This helps AI businesses such as OpenAI pay their salaries, and acquire tools, servers and processors – and, at the backend of this business success, also helps them raise more capital from investors in their move towards AGI.
- **Help the rich make life easier:** The second big move is to help those with money live easier lives. If AI can be used to sell expensive toys, solutions and household robots to families with cash, it can open up a new revenue stream to take more cash from the rich in pursuit of doing good for the whole. These amazing robots that everyone can have at home, for example, will start at $30 000 and then gradually be made available to the masses at a more affordable price – but in the early stages, only a few will be able to enjoy them. This is yet another way to pay the bills and instil confidence in AGI.
- **Help society advance in leaps and bounds:** In the last phase of deployment, although it may not be as linear as described here, OpenAI and other big AI companies will have already landed on AGI. At this point, we expect computers to be so intelligent and computing power to be so available that the masses can finally benefit from the greater promises of AI – that is, 'that AI can solve all the world's problems', in more or less the words of Sam Altman.

But while we will have incredible insights, data and even wisdom in this final stage of AGI, the only real question is whether humans will be prepared to evolve with it. AI may provide all the best options for a decision in a particular set of circumstances, but a person still has to act on that decision. Some AI solutions will be obvious, have social impact and be massively profitable for the stakeholders involved. If a company such as Neuralink can help every blind human see again, that's life-changing for the blind community and a massive new revenue stream for Elon Musk and others in this space. But other solutions will be less obvious, have less social impact and not be so profitable for people in power. If we can solve cancer by zapping bad cells at a molecular level with AI precision tools in just one treatment, that is incredibly great for society but not so good for the multi-billion-dollar chemotherapy industry. AI agents will come up with great solutions, but someone in charge still has to decide whether or not to move forward with those solutions.

We already live in a world where there are enough resources for every human to live well. There are vast supplies of food, water, land and material in the ground for everyone to have a home and achieve a good quality of life that offers access to all the basic things they will ever need. As per the United Nations Food Waste Index Report of 2024, one-fifth of food produced for human consumption is lost or wasted globally. This amounts to one billion meals a day. That is enough to feed every person on the African continent, every day! Elon Musk recently said that drinking water is not scarce – we just haven't figured out desalination yet (how to take sea salt out of water). How can water be scarce on a planet that is 70% covered by it? The only reason we have not really solved this by now is that those of us who have the resources to research and solve this challenge currently live in big cities, where we can simply turn on a tap and get the water we need, or run to the grocery store to buy millions of plastic bottles, so it is not really a priority for us right now.

So the resources and solutions are already there, and always have been. The answers to the world's problems were there way before AI was even conceived. Our only real dilemma has always been whether we would equitably distribute our resources. This isn't a matter of logic or science, nor is it a matter of capitalism or communism. There are many models for everyone to have the basics and some to have more, if they work for it. The only question is how much is enough. This is simply a matter of giving vs. hoarding, kindness vs. greed, love vs. fear. To make real human leaps, we will need far more than AI: we will need a shift in human consciousness. But even so, AI can prove to be really useful in the short term and it's worth looking at what that might mean.

EVOLUTION OF AI IN THE WORLD: THE FOUR PLAYERS

AI's evolution will not unfold in some obvious and predictable way. It depends on the ambitions of those who create it, the desires of those who consume it and the laws of those who govern it. In the short term, societies will take different approaches – some might sacrifice economic progress to preserve heritage, while others will pursue AI dominance at the cost of chaos. This means some countries might struggle before things improve globally. But, in the long run, our differences will align and everyone will benefit. Whether it takes 20 or 200 years, a better future awaits us all. Let's explore the four main players driving AI's future and their unique motivations.

Player 1: Companies

Some companies focus on cutting costs – at any cost. The few that run and benefit from a venture's success may be happy to cut unnecessary people and activities out everywhere just to increase their margins. Other companies know that their people are key to their success, so they will free up time for staff from mundane activities and let them focus on building better relationships and products or spend time doing what they do best. Then there are public companies with shareholder needs. If these companies replace their staff with robots, the extra cash saved by automating the workforce will end up back in the bank – and shareholders will demand that this capital be reinvested or used efficiently. This means that companies that save excess cash have room to launch new businesses, products and markets, and then you need people all over again. So as AI gets implemented by these different types of companies, there may or may not be new jobs coming from them.

Player 2: AI inventors

The people building and spreading the tech all have different motivations too. Some are doing it for status, money, human progress, intellectual competition or plain fear of falling behind. Others are doing it for a combination of these reasons. But what we don't realize is that AI isn't something that just happens to us; rather, we are creating it. People like us are just sitting around in their living rooms or at their desks or in their beds thinking about what to build, how to build it and what next move makes the most sense. In some cases you have wacky scientists who want to play god and create machines that may be better than humans. Larry Page, co-founder of Google, is known for thinking that machines may be more deserving of running society than we are. On the other hand, Ilya Sutskever is known for quitting his job at OpenAI/ChatGPT and wanting to start his own company that focuses on AI safety and on making sure machines do not take over. The sum of all these activities is our shared future as well as our different futures based on where and how these inventors launch their ideas.

Player 3: Governments

Each country also decides how far AI will go. The European Union has taken a stance on preserving culture and valuing human life. As a result, they are not investing heavily in AI or passing any law that makes AI ubiquitous. Currently, they are criticized for 'being so antiquated' because it prevents economic progress and potential job prosperity in new AI fields and investments. But if they maintain a healthy version of this stance and invest in some AI to keep abreast of human progress, while also preserving human culture, then this could become good for the economy in a different way. For example, the last truly human societies might come to be in demand in a different way from highly technological societies. Even now, the migration from the busy and high-rise life in New York or Toronto to the small, quiet and quaint towns of Italy and Portugal is already a massive market. People too often think in binary terms, while in reality things are seldom that simple. Some countries, by contrast, want to double down on AI as a war tool. Every time a nation gains access to a new technology, they use it to enforce control over other nations instead of pursuing collective prosperity with them. In other words, many countries are still motivated by fear rather than collective progress.

Player 4: Customers, citizens, humans

The world is one giant economy and economies run on markets, and markets are driven by customers. Everything is always cyclical – not linear. People get smartphones and then they want dumb phones; people get MP3 players and then they want record players; people get digital books and then they want go back to hard-copy books – and so people will love and get comfortable with robots and then soon crave human connection again, and the imperfection of humans. And so money will always flow where people continue to seek out human-centred needs. But some activities will be linear: no one will stop using a crane out of nostalgia for carrying rocks on their shoulders again like the slaves in ancient Egypt. Some humans might find it a beautiful meditative practice to clean the house, but it's hard to think that all the world's toilet cleaners will miss their work once they have been educated into new lifestyles. So, while old-school will be very attractive, many of us are also excited for the next world. We do want to buy new iPads, iPhones, virtual-reality glasses, robots and trips to space. Some of us are fully and deeply invested in this new future, some of us want that plain life in nature, and others want a combination. This will also, or mainly, drive the design of new futures and societies.

But there is always an organic interplay between all these variables and players: human progress isn't neatly organized. Elon Musk might push for a certain future as he sees it in his mind, but it's only as possible as it is palatable. Customers need to buy Teslas, Optimus robots and SpaceX cargo loads to keep the vision moving. Governments need to sign Musk's contracts and give him innovation tax breaks to make sure he gets to space. The world's best engineers need to believe in Musk to work for him and make his feats possible – it's all connected. But even with a smooth train of events such as this one, everything can also change overnight. A new US president might come in, see robots taking over, and choose to tax every family that owns a robot and require every citizen to make a new annual tax contribution towards universal basic income (UBI). People might then protest, more jobs would be lost and UBI may not come to fruition. This could slow down robot acquisitions, create new factions in the US economy and even give rise to US states that are 'robot-free' and 'non-UBI-taxed'. These states could even inadvertently become safe havens from robot takeovers or become places where ancient traditions, low-tech living and holistic human values are honoured. Things will also evolve at a rate that is related to other variables: energy, computer processing power and cost of labour. But whatever it is, the future will be a dynamic and ever-changing affair, and we will need to be mentally prepared for all kinds of scenarios to succeed in our businesses and careers.

THE FIVE FUTURES

These are the futures and their ensuing scenarios that could drive what the world looks like next over this coming decade. In each scenario you will see that technologists, governments and societies simply have different views, values and responses based on how AI is unfolding.

The UBI future

Universal basic income is a financial programme in which all citizens receive a regular, unconditional sum of money from the government, regardless of employment status. The idea is to provide a safety net, reduce poverty and promote financial stability in an economy that becomes increasingly influenced by automation and AI. In this scenario, the government, alongside producers, realizes that there will be a gap between the current economic position and future economic prosperity for all. To fill this gap, the government uses its reserves and introduces basic pay to keep spending going in the economy and help the masses by providing a basic livelihood. UBI ensures that even those who lose their jobs can still purchase goods and services, to keep the economy stable.

But what's really interesting about how companies shape the world is that they have to work together with governments to influence policy development. To ensure that AI has a chance to live up to its promises, Sam Altman of OpenAI actually launched a UBI experiment, among others that he plans to fund, to see how

UBI should be structured to help society make a leap. These experiments involve funding pilot programmes in various regions to assess UBI's effects on poverty alleviation, economic stability and job creation. Based on the results of these experiments, the government may make it easier for Altman and other AI influencers to do their work at scale or even fund some of their projects. These experiments also give the government a chance to gather data and optimistic insights to plan their own rollout of UBI when it will be needed.

But the vision for the long-term scenario is that AI financial gains in the economy can actually be used to fund UBI – meaning companies that replace humans with robots to save money might also have to pay a tax to the government for each human replaced, into perpetuity. This is a win–win for companies and society, because the corporation saves on paying a human to do the job but also pays a percentage of those savings to the government for someone at home to chill and buy groceries and pay rent. This scenario will probably only work if the corporation is paying a tax that equates to 20% to 30% of the human salary saved, so in a ratio of 1:1, which means that if every human were to be replaced by a robot, then each human that was getting paid $3 000 to work would get paid $1 000 to not work. The tax policy might even extend in its definition as companies and economies become more prosperous. If a robot not only saves costs but also makes more revenue, then, for every time a robot doubles the revenue you used to make with a human in that position, you might be taxed another $2 000 per robot per month. This ensures that people who lost their jobs are not just making ends meet with their measly $1 000, but rather getting back to what they were originally earning and possibly even more in the future.

As the United States advances in AI and considers UBI, it may benefit significantly from increased productivity and reduced poverty. However, countries such as India and South Africa could face challenges. They may experience job displacement owing to AI without the financial safety net that UBI offers. African or Asian governments may not have the financial infrastructure or private-sector support to make UBI a reality in those economies. Also, in the short term, human labour may still remain cheaper than robots, so people will not lose their jobs, but in the long run, as automation spreads, these countries could start seeing increased unemployment for a certain period until their governments can properly tax local corporations for robot use. As AI and automation transform the economy, countries will need to work together and come up with creative policies to ensure that everyone benefits fairly from these advancements.

The household robot future

In this future, middle- to upper-income households own humanoid robots designed to handle domestic tasks such as cooking, cleaning, childcare and home maintenance. These robots perform errands, manage schedules and assist with healthcare monitoring, freeing people to pursue personal goals, careers or leisure activities. For example, a parent with a demanding job might rely on the robot to prepare meals and help children with homework. People in this scenario experience better work–life balance, engage in lifelong learning, and spend more time with family and friends. Robots also help reduce stress by eliminating routine tasks, creating a society where time is reinvested into personal development and wellbeing.

However, this convenience comes at a cost. Low- and middle-skill workers, including domestic workers, delivery personnel and maintenance staff, are displaced by robots. Those unable to afford robots face a growing inequality gap. Many previously essential jobs are eliminated, and entire segments of the population could struggle to find employment. At this stage there may not be a UBI but rather an extensive social welfare grant for all people who immediately lose their jobs to household robots. A tax on household robots will probably not be applied, as that will dissuade end customers from buying a robot in the first place. In the early stages, AI companies that sell robots might have to give a portion of their earnings, over and above regular tax, to the government to assist with funding these social welfare grants. This would create a two-tier society: those who own robots and benefit from AI-driven efficiency, and those who rely on public programmes to survive. This economy showcases both the promise and peril of automation: improved wellbeing for some, but deeper social divisions if access to these technologies is unevenly distributed.

However, developing economies such as Africa will continue to have a large pool of low-cost labour willing to perform tasks that robots would automate, such as manufacturing, farming and domestic work. This makes it economically sensible for businesses to hire humans rather than invest in automation. The infrastructure to support advanced robotic systems might also not be available – such as reliable electricity and internet connectivity. That's why Tesla didn't enter the South African market for a long time despite consumer demand – there is no point in owning a Tesla in an economy that struggles with electricity. Many companies may prioritize gradual improvements before fully embracing robots. As a result, human labour will likely continue to play a significant role in these economies in the near term, despite the possibility of automation in the future.

The meaningful work future

In this future, AI takes over mechanical jobs such as factory work, administration and entry-level roles, allowing humans to focus on more creative, emotional and strategic work. Even when we reach

AGI, we might realize that AI is still only a powerful collaborator and not a competitor, helping people make better decisions rather than being the final decision-makers. This is why Roelof Botha, who runs renowned venture capital firm Sequoia Capital, says that AI should probably stand for *augmented intelligence* rather than artificial intelligence, because it seems as though AI will be more about *helping* than *replacing*. In this future people might also get to pursue more careers that resonate with their passions, values and talents. Social impact could become the centre of the work experience, meaning people won't work for companies that sell unhealthy, environmentally unfriendly and soulless goods. People will get to choose where they work and so they will be more deliberate about applying their expertise to companies that make a difference in the world.

Now, from where we currently stand, this might seem too utopian to be true, but it is actually quite a plausible future, which could happen in two stages. First, it could take a long time before AI eats up many highly skilled roles, so, until these workers get laid off, the government can work on creating a solid UBI plan for those low-skilled workers who will have lost their jobs much sooner. But what might happen next is that many high-skill workers will eventually lose their jobs to AI too and start living off UBI. During this period, these very talented people could upskill and become creative in new ways, and many could even start new kinds of ventures that might become very successful. Big corporations, which would have been largely automated, will notice these new trends and plan their next market moves. They might realize that they need to hire skilled workers once again to reinvent themselves for even newer futures. But to attract top talent in a world where people do not have to work for their basic living expenses, these giants might have to design new roles in collaboration with their next employees. They might have to consider new ways to attract a conscious workforce and build social impact into their future business models.

The post-money future

In this future, AI has advanced to a level where it autonomously manages most industries and services, creating a post-work society in which human labour is largely unnecessary. Manufacturing, transportation, agriculture and even healthcare operate with minimal human involvement, as AI systems and robotics handle most tasks. In this society there is so much prosperity that people have what Elon Musk calls a universal high income (UHI) as opposed to UBI. In other words, if UBI paid your rent, groceries and internet bill so that you could just stay at home all day and play video games, UHI would give you the chance to buy more experiences, travel the world and live with more luxury. There are a few interesting ways in which this would be made possible:

- **Unlimited raw material:** We literally live off rocks and minerals in the ground. Everything that you call the habitable world and the things within it was once barren land or a jungle with animals. So where did all these riches and niceties come from? The ground, obviously. But in a world where people colonized and took ownership of ground, or property, you now have all the essential rock, stone and mineral owned by a few, in service of the whole. Many underdeveloped societies and governments also have many great resources but do not have the infrastructure or knowledge to mine their own 'gold'. So they outsource it to European or US companies at a massive cost; they almost give away ownership – and therefore never let their own people rise above their basic means. But in a knowledge- and machine-abundant future, we can expect this all to change. For one thing, machines could be used to build other machines. Fleets of robots could be used to build mining infrastructure and even mine for us. Mining could also happen at a much faster rate, giving more to those that never had. But even more interestingly, AI and advanced robots could give us access to raw materials beyond the earth, especially as SpaceX builds reusable rockets so quickly. If rock and metal and iron are all we need, then we can get tons of each from neighbouring planets. We can even mine asteroids that are big enough to provide for the needs of multiple generations of humans – and they're just out there, floating, belonging to no one except those interested in taking a chunk. But because there is so much available, even if those humans in power are still greedy, it will not knock a percentage off their balance sheets to help every human get everything they need, at ultra-low cost. In this future, the global powerhouses will probably be more interested in colonizing other planets than hanging out here and begging for your pennies.

- **Unlimited production**: With cheaper raw materials come cheaper production costs. But as robots will be doing almost everything, you will also have accelerated production cycles. You will now effectively live in a world where there are lots of goods and they are being made extremely fast. The world would be reminiscent of Chinese company Temu, which has been flooding African markets. Whether their current practices are environmentally sustainable or ethical is a separate affair, but their slogan cleverly sums up this concept: 'Shop like a billionaire'. Their customers are largely surprised at how much they can get with so little, which is what makes the Temu shopping experience exciting and accessible to the masses. But we also see this low-cost movement happening in other product categories. What we used to consider luxury vehicles were simply limited to the ingenuity and high material costs of the great Italian and German brands. Now Japanese and Indian and Korean companies are figuring out their own ways to make equally beautiful and functional cars – at a fraction of the cost of a BMW or a Porsche, so the state of all cars is already looking far more luxurious than in previous decades. We're also starting to see behind the veil of luxury goods companies such as Louis Vuitton and Gucci. All those products we thought were so expensive to make are turning out to be cheaper than our average lunch. As a global society we are becoming aware of how accessible things are and can be in ways we never knew before. If this is already happening now, then post-AI you can expect the world to be very cheap, and you can expect to start enjoying the experience of being human, no matter where you are or how much you were born into – and that's truly exciting.

- **Synthesizing goods**: One of the most notable features of the TV series *Star Trek*, which has been such a huge inspiration for so many modern-day inventors, including Jeff Bezos and Steve Jobs, is the 'replicator'. This is a machine that can create anything you want by simply converting energy into matter. Imagine it being like the microwave in the kitchen, except that on the display screen you can enter anything you want to create. Then, within minutes, it appears in the microwave and you simply open the door to take it out. But this is not some magical affair: it is pure science. All matter can be broken down into its simplest form, atoms. And replicators simply rearrange atoms to produce the matter that you wish to create. This technology comes from an area of study called quantum physics. And right now, across the world, especially in Canada, billions are being spent on research and advancing the state of quantum computing. These research labs, which employ some of the most brilliant minds, are already attempting to make massive leaps towards what they call the quantum future, by 2100 – which is only 75 years away – a future some of our children and grandchildren will live in. And on the basis of success in quantum computing, we will not be far from replicating goods and services by rearranging and manipulating atoms. When this will be achieved is unclear, but that it will be achieved is absolutely certain. With AI tools, we can increase our computing power by such a high exponent that our research in these new areas is not limited to the daily grind of 100 or 1 000 scientists showing up to a lab every day. AI will be like one million scientists showing up to every lab every day – and with that computing power, there is great speed and certainty for great success. We may soon reach a future where everyone can have everything they want – from food to medicine and machinery – thereby relinquishing the need for cash and allowing us to truly enter a post-money society.

The spiritual future

In a world of material abundance, where humanity no longer worries about basic needs, a new challenge might emerge: the loss of existential meaning. With physical survival secured and work no longer necessary, people might struggle to find purpose. This future will require humanity to explore deeper questions about life and identity – potentially beginning a new society-wide search for spiritual meaning. Based on Maslow's hierarchy of needs, we will ultimately have everything we need, so self-actualization or the search for something higher would become our next focus. As people have more free time, it will become clear that entertainment alone cannot fill the void of existence. This spiritual era would therefore represent a deeper realization and remind people that life's meaning is not in what we produce or consume, but in how we connect and grow.

It's generally unclear how these futures will all pan out, but they are likely to take place in the order presented here. The elements of each future will probably mix and match with other futures; it's not a cookie-cutter roadmap to the future. But naturally, we can expect many low-skill workers to lose jobs first, UBI to be released next to combat the effects of that, then some high-skill workers to lose jobs thereafter, and then new economies to emerge and meaningful work to be on the rise – although survival could still be a theme for these eras if UBI doesn't cover everyone. Finally, cheap goods can be expected, no matter what, UBI will eventually become possible with all the economic gains and taxes that governments earn from highly profitable AI companies, and the post-money future will not be far off. Then, once cash is no longer the goal, and work is no longer necessary, every human will be in search of greater life meaning. We will then need to redefine the terms of engagement on earth and the meaning of being human in the grand scheme of the universe. But for now, we just need to figure out what our next jobs are going to be.

MENTAL MODELS

- **The AI inventors' roadmap:** Getting to AGI is expensive, so companies developing the most advanced AI need a good plan to fund their journey. It can be summarized as first, *helping companies get rich* (AI for business productivity, cost cutting and revenue gains); secondly, *helping the rich save time* (AI to make personal life easy at home, for example by owning a robot maid for $30 000); and thirdly, *helping society advance in leaps and bounds* (using AI to help the masses, giving everyone a great free version of ChatGPT now, but also helping everyone get access to quantum computing power and almost free goods and services in the future).

- **The four players**: The ultimate destination of AI is prosperity for all, if things go as optimistically expected. But the journey there is shaped and influenced by four players: companies, AI inventors, governments and citizens. Together they work in an organic and dynamic relationship, affecting each other's decisions and creating the 'future', of which there may be different kinds for different people, based on where they live and what they predominantly believe.

- **The five futures**: The AI future has different stages of development but also different economic themes. It's unclear how it will all pan out, or whether it will pan out in a linear way, but what we know is that the five big themes or stages of economic development in the AI era are the UBI future, the household robot future, the meaningful work future, the post-money future and the spiritual future.

PART 3
JOBS

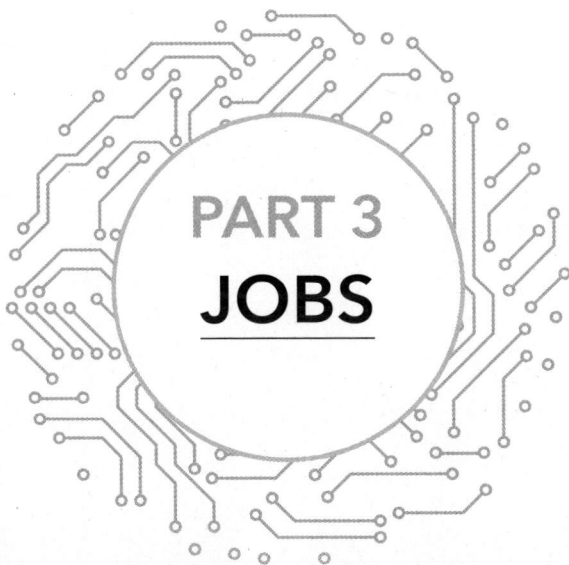

As long as there is human desire, there are jobs. And humans have insatiable desires, imaginations, curiosities and dreams. Pay attention to that and you'll never be without a job.

8

HOW WILL AI AFFECT MY ROLE?

In 2020, the World Economic Forum wrote: 'By 2025, automation and a new division of labour between humans and machines will disrupt 85 million jobs globally in medium and large businesses across 15 industries and 26 economies.' But also: 'As the economy and job markets evolve, 97 million new roles will emerge.' This future is already unfolding, and while the actual job numbers might look different, what we know for sure is that the main idea is largely true. Yes, jobs have been replaced, but also, yes, more jobs have been created. While this is mythical for most, like a black box with empty dreams, the advancement of AI in the economy is actually quite predictable. Based on how AI is evolving, we can logically see how jobs will be automated, augmented and reinvented. Here is a look at the phases of this evolution.

- Imagine that every job – whether in sales, marketing or design, from entry level to director – has around ten main responsibilities.

- These responsibilities can be stacked on a ladder, ranging from repetitive and tactical at the bottom to case sensitive and strategic at the top.
- Lower on the ladder, where activities and outcomes are highly predictable, the potential for automation is higher.
- Higher on the ladder, where tasks involve less predictability and more nuanced decision making, automation potential decreases.
- At the bottom of the ladder, machines can handle almost 100% of repetitive responsibilities independently.
- As you move higher up the ladder, there is more collaboration between humans and machines, with machines performing a smaller share of the total workload.
- At the highest levels, humans take the lead in strategic, creative or emotionally sensitive responsibilities, while machines assist by automating routine or analytical tasks.

Let's look at three roles – sales, graphic design and HR recruiting – to see how this could work in practice. Note the percentage distribution between human involvement and machine involvement. As AI improves, the distributions will increasingly change, with machines becoming more involved than humans at each level of responsibility, but not necessarily ever replacing humans completely. This table ranks the tasks from least easy to automate at the top to most easy to automate at the bottom.

Tasks	Sales	Graphic design	HR recruiting	Machine involvement (%)	Human involvement (%)
Strategic (less automatable)	Building client relationships	Crafting brand identities	Designing long-term hiring strategies	10%	90%
	Designing sales strategies	Creating original concepts	Managing executive hiring	20%	80%
	Negotiating high-value contracts	Overseeing product launch designs	Handling complex employee disputes	15%	85%
Partially automatable	Analysing sales trends	Collaborating on campaigns	Reviewing applications with AI tools	40%	60%
	Personalizing offers based on customer data	Refining AI-generated designs	Conducting initial interview screenings	50%	50%
	Coordinating between departments	Creating mock-ups with templates	Managing candidate databases	60%	40%
Repetitive (highly automatable)	Data entry into CRM (customer relationship management)	Resizing and formatting images	Scheduling interviews	90%	10%
	Auto-sending follow-up emails	Auto-generating templates	Sending job-offer letters	85%	15%
	Scheduling meetings	Background removal	Generating automated rejection emails	80%	20%

PERCENTAGE OF ROLE THAT IS REPLACED BY AI

While AI can technically replace many roles, whether or not it will actually replace them is based on government policy, cost of labour, company values, cost of technology, availability of electricity, customer attitude towards humans as opposed to machines and the speed to reach AGI. This means that various things need to be aligned for a full-scale robot takeover. But there is one thing we can be certain of, according to Demis Hassabis, who runs Google's AI arm, DeepMind Technologies, and recently won a Nobel Prize for his work in AI: AGI should only arrive by 2035. That means many uniquely human skills and socially nuanced tasks will still be better exercised by humans than computers. Even if Hassabis was conservative in his prediction and doubled the time, AGI would still only arrive by 2030. This gives society a decent amount of time to get comfortable with AI, double down on uniquely human skills and prepare for life on the other side.

So let's look at some specific roles across a variety of industries to get a sense of what percentage of an *entire role* could be automated. This percentage differs slightly from the above table, which showed us how much of each job responsibility within a role could be automated. Why is this useful? It is the perfect time to get clear, in no uncertain terms, where you are most replaceable in your role, and then to double down on being the best in those areas in which you are not easy to replace. As time frees up for you, don't assume your employers are happy for you to have longer lunches, either. The idea of getting more free time because robots are doing all the work is more true for business owners than employees. It's the owners who get to chill out more in this case. It may be true that you get free time when you go home to a beautifully cleaned house courtesy of your Tesla robot, but at work you will have to show that you are adding more value to your company during the increasing number of saved hours. This cannot be an attempt to work harder to fill space, but to provide more value in your role and keep your job, as AI increasingly eats up more of your tasks. So, the final column lists some ideas on where to shift your focus next within your role.

ChatGPT was used to create this table and to provide a broad view across diverse roles. If your role was not included here, you can use ChatGPT to get more specific insights into your particular job area. Look not only at 'what cannot be automated or how to use freed-up time', but also at the skills you will need to complete new kinds of tasks and how to educate yourself next. We look at this in more detail in 'Your guide to getting started with AI' at the end of this book. But in case you find it useful, this is what I put into ChatGPT to come up with this table. You can use and amend the words to get answers that are more specific to your situation. I used the following prompt:

Create a table showing ten different jobs across ten industries, highlighting their potential for automation. For each role, include:
- *the percentage of the role that can be automated*
- *tasks that can be automated*
- *tasks that cannot be automated*
- *how to use the freed-up time in ways that are valuable for the company.*

Job	Automation potential (%)	Tasks that can be automated	Tasks that cannot be easily automated	Valuable use of freed-up time
Lawyer at big law firm	40%–50%	Contract review, legal research, document drafting, e-discovery	Negotiation, courtroom presence, advising on complex legal issues	Focusing on high-level strategy, client relations, thought leadership
Consultant at McKinsey	30%–40%	Data collection, modelling, report generation	Strategic advice, client meetings, stakeholder management	Building stronger client networks, deepening industry expertise
Investment banker at Goldman Sachs	35%–50%	Financial modelling, due diligence, transaction monitoring	Deal negotiation, relationship management, client acquisition	Relationship building with investors, creating new financial products
HR onboarding at Google	60%–70%	Résumé screening, interview scheduling, paperwork processing	Employee engagement, onboarding experience, resolving issues	Focusing on employee-retention strategies, improving work culture
Professor at Harvard	20%–30%	Grading, course scheduling, virtual office hours automation	Teaching, mentoring, research, fostering discussions	Writing research papers, mentoring students, networking with industry
Doctor at Mayo Clinic	30%–40%	Data entry, diagnostics via AI tools, appointment scheduling	Surgery, patient interaction, complex diagnosis	Research, personalized patient care, medical innovation
Designer at Tesla	40%–50%	Prototyping, repetitive visual tasks, design mock-ups	Conceptual design, brain-storming sessions, user experience refinement	Focusing on innovation, user testing, improving aesthetics
Accountant at PwC	70%–80%	Data entry, audit processes, tax preparation	Financial analysis, illogical fraud detection, advisory roles	Business development, strengthening client relationships

Job	Automation potential (%)	Tasks that can be automated	Tasks that cannot be easily automated	Valuable use of freed-up time
Engineer at NASA	20%–30%	Simulation, data processing, technical documentation	Designing missions, research on space technologies	Innovating in space exploration, mentoring young engineers
Surgeon at Johns Hopkins	20%–30%	Scheduling, diagnostic assistance through AI	Surgery, patient care, complex decision making	Advancing surgical techniques, mentoring younger professionals

FUTURE OF CURRENT INDUSTRIES

With more free time emerging as AI increasingly replaces more of your responsibilities, you will find it helpful to think about the future of your current role. Remember the promise of AI is not that we simply get to work on the things that we enjoy more, but also on the things that matter more in the world. In the automation potential table, we can see that humans are doing less repetitive tasks and more strategic and creative work. This is already exciting. But what is even more exciting is that you will be able to work on completely new ideas. All over the world right now there are meetings happening in all kinds of companies and departments, many of which end with great ideas that those teams will never get to execute. There is always an 'imagine we could do this' conversation. But long before the idea gets any fuel, people are back at the demands of their current tasks. We could call these ideas 'moonshot ideas': they are the big-thinking ideas that can redefine companies and industries, and even move the world forward. Every company is uniquely positioned to bring these ideas to life. So the next big promise of AI is that we will have freed up so much time that we can finally get to new things that matter. Here is a view of what this could look like in the same industries we just reviewed.

Moonshot idea by industry	Detailed explanation of moonshot	New responsibilities
Law: AI-driven global legal frameworks	Imagine an AI that handles international contracts and legal cases instantly, harmonizing laws across countries. Companies could avoid legal disputes with auto-generated contracts that align with regulations globally. Disputes are resolved in real time, reducing the need for lengthy legal processes.	Focusing on negotiation and advocacy in complex disputes, interpreting AI regulations, and building trust with clients in emotionally charged cases
Consulting: Predicting global market shifts	AI systems continuously analyse economic trends, social behaviours and geopolitical factors, giving companies advanced insights into future opportunities or risks. Consulting firms could become less reactive and more proactive, guiding clients through predicted downturns before they occur.	Synthesizing AI insights for clients, developing long-term strategies and managing ethical challenges related to AI-driven forecasting
Banking: Creating alternative currencies	Banks could issue cryptocurrencies as standard offerings to replace traditional cross-border transactions. A new financial era might emerge, where borderless currencies reduce transaction times, enable financial inclusion and redefine wealth distribution.	Educating clients about digital currencies, collaborating with regulators to develop frameworks and managing cybersecurity risks for financial technologies
HR: Personalized AI-driven career coaching	AI career coaches provide employees with dynamic development plans, guiding their growth paths while monitoring mental health. AI will recommend new skills to learn, offer role transitions and even design wellbeing plans, turning HR into a personalized support function.	Curating cultural programmes and adapting wellbeing strategies to complement AI-driven recommendations
Academia: AI-powered global classrooms	Universities could leverage AI tools to deliver personalized education to students around the world. AI-driven platforms will monitor student performance and offer tailored feedback, removing geographical barriers to education. Professors could manage global classrooms with ease, providing mentorship on demand.	Teaching critical thinking beyond AI's reach and leading cross-cultural collaboration projects
Healthcare: Preventive healthcare platforms	Wearable technology powered by AI will track patients' vitals and predict potential illnesses in advance, shifting healthcare from reactive treatment to prevention. Patients could receive real-time advice through apps to reduce unnecessary hospital visits.	Interpreting health data, developing personalized treatment strategies and building relationships with patients to enhance preventive care

Moonshot idea by industry	Detailed explanation of moonshot	New responsibilities
Design: Self-evolving, sustainable designs	Products will evolve autonomously based on user behaviour and environmental conditions. Cars, buildings or appliances might update themselves to remain efficient, reducing waste and extending product lifespans. Designers will focus on integrating sustainable innovations and aesthetics into these self-adapting systems.	Conceptualizing creative design ideas, collaborating with AI systems and ensuring sustainable development
Accounting: Real-time auditing with AI	Auditing firms could use AI to conduct continuous, real-time audits, detecting financial irregularities and fraud instantly. This shift would eliminate traditional auditing cycles and improve financial transparency.	Handling nuanced financial cases, interpreting anomalies and advising clients on long-term financial strategy
Engineering: Asteroid mining for resources	Robotic miners could harvest rare minerals from asteroids, providing earth with abundant resources or fuelling space missions. This could spark a new era of space exploration and off-planet manufacturing that will transform the economy and reduce material shortages.	Designing robotic systems for space operations, coordinating international policies and exploring sustainable solutions for off-earth resource use
Surgery: Autonomous robotic surgeries	Robotic systems could take over routine surgeries, allowing for faster and safer procedures. Surgeons would focus on complex cases and emotional care, guiding patients before and after surgery. This could make healthcare more efficient and accessible.	Managing complex surgical cases, handling patient relationships and making critical decisions during unforeseen events

NEW ROLES AS A RESULT OF AI

The next thing we can look forward to is the invention of new roles as a result of the AI industry. Many proponents of AI, such as Jonathan Ross from Groq and Sam Altman from OpenAI, say that AI may cause some disruptions in the labour market in the short term but then provide many new opportunities in the long term. But based on what I wrote in earlier chapters, there is no real disruption for people who keep educating themselves and reinventing their roles to meet the gaps, demands and needs of a new world. So while we can expect abundant opportunity in existing industries, there will also be many new exciting industries to look forward to that are centred on the AI revolution. Here is a view of some of the technical, non-technical and emerging roles that AI will create or enhance.

Non-technical AI roles: Human skills in a digital world

Not all future AI-related roles will require programming expertise. AI opens up opportunities in human-centric fields that depend on unique human skills and specialized knowledge.

- **AI ethicists and policy advisors:** These experts will navigate the moral and regulatory aspects of AI's growing influence to help ensure the technology serves society fairly and transparently.
- **Storytellers and AI content curators:** With generative AI creating stories, music and art, human storytellers will play a key role in curating, refining and aligning content with cultural and emotional needs.
- **Mental health professionals specializing in AI-related issues:** As AI increases its impact on work–life dynamics, therapists and counsellors will address anxiety about automation, job loss or digital dependency.

Technical AI roles: New opportunities in engineering and data science

New technologies will be accompanied by new opportunities to build, improve and maintain those technologies.

- **AI trainers and model curators:** These trainers will feed datasets into AI systems, improve models with feedback and fine-tune them based on industry needs.
- **AI safety specialists:** These social-science and engineering

thinkers will focus on ensuring that advanced AI systems remain aligned with human values and operate without causing harm.

- **Robotics engineers**: To meet increased demand for automation, engineers will design AI-powered robots for the entire economy.

Bioengineering, cloning and physiological enhancements: Beyond traditional industries

New tools will be accompanied by new human experiments. AI will also be used in bioengineering, gene editing and human-enhancement technologies. Neuralink is the start, but this game can become excessive.

- **Bioengineers developing smart prosthetics**: These professionals will design AI-driven prosthetics and implants to enhance physical abilities.
- **Cloning and genetic modification experts**: AI will help scientists explore cloning and genetic editing with greater precision, which will lead to roles in gene therapy and human-enhancement research.
- **Creative superhumans**: Advances in brain–computer interfaces could unlock new ways for humans to enhance cognitive abilities, creativity or memory to create entirely new roles in human–computer interaction design – or quite simply be the beginning of superman.

New industries emerging from AI: The unseen opportunities

AI will also drive the creation of whole new industries that we can't yet fully envision.

- **Immersive virtual worlds**: AI will allow for hyperrealistic virtual spaces that can be used in education, entertainment and therapy, thereby generating roles such as virtual experience designers or metaverse architects.

- **Astrobiology and space mining engineers**: As AI accelerates space exploration, new roles will emerge to mine resources on asteroids or explore interstellar ecosystems.

TIME AND MONEY FOR IMPORTANT PROBLEMS

For a long time, and perhaps for the entire time, AI will prove to be a replacer of routine roles but primarily an augmenter of strategic, creative and problem-solving roles. This means that, as AI frees up more time in existing industries, more people may have fractional strategic or creative roles across multiple enterprises. In other words, if you are a designer, engineer, copywriter or salesperson, at some point in the future you might only be required in the office for 1.5 days a week. Your bosses will be happy with AI's performance with the rest of the tasks you used to do and now you will come in only to be the bigger brain behind AI. But if at this point UBI does not exist in your country or if it doesn't cover all your expenses, you will have the opportunity to work in some of the newer, more important industries that are on the rise. You will play a fractional strategy role in three companies, each only requiring 1.5 days a week from you, and that is how you will fill your work week.

This is great; like this, you get to work only on the best stuff, you have a variety of projects, and you are using your talents and passions to solve some of the most important problems in the world. In the context of all the global changes we are experiencing right now, many of the United Nations Sustainable Development Goals (SDGs) are related to challenges that need to be solved. Billions of dollars of investment are going towards those SDGs. Markets for climate-related solutions, such as renewable energy and water desalination, are expanding rapidly. For example, the voluntary carbon market alone now features over 850 active projects, with more than 2 000 in development that are generating billions in economic opportunities (see, for example, IFC.org). In 2024, cumulative investments in climate-focused initiatives and carbon-reduction efforts were expected to exceed $15 billion. These developments offer an exciting opportunity for investors, businesses and individuals to participate in shaping a more sustainable world. Here is a brief overview of what we can expect next.

Climate change and the green economy

One of the most pressing global challenges is climate change. AI can help monitor environmental changes and create predictive models for disaster response, but human intervention is crucial for systemic change. As we gain more time to focus on policy and innovation, we can develop green economies and industries that focus on sustainable practices. Jobs could emerge in fields such as renewable energy consulting, carbon capture and urban agriculture – all essential in addressing environmental degradation.

Circular economy and sustainability thinking

As we transition from a linear economy – focused on production, use and disposal – towards a circular economy, innovation will play a key role in rethinking how we design, manufacture and recycle products. This shift requires deeper thinking in materials science, waste management and sustainable design. As AI is focused on the basics, humans can focus on rethinking consumption patterns and designing products that last longer or can be recycled efficiently. Sustainability professionals, including environmental engineers and eco-educators, will consult with businesses to develop eco-friendly solutions and shift mindsets towards a more regenerative economic system.

Reforming the criminal justice system

AI's ability to handle administrative tasks opens the door for deeper discussions around criminal justice reform. Rather than functioning solely as punitive institutions, prisons can evolve into rehabilitation centres integrated with society, where the focus is on skills training, mental health support and reintegration programmes. This means that policymakers, social workers and mental health professionals could focus on designing evidence-based rehabilitation programmes. If AI systems support parole assessments and track re-entry programmes, the justice system could shift towards reducing repeat offender rates and fostering a culture of second chances.

Improving education for everyone

As AI takes over tasks such as grading, scheduling and attendance tracking, teachers can shift their focus towards more meaningful and effective work. They'll have more time to mentor and coach students in areas that demand empathy and emotional intelligence, such as how to manage interviews, engage in honest relationships and foster healthy team dynamics. Educators will also play a significant role in developing strategies to make education more inclusive and personalized, and ensuring that every student can be successful in a changing world. The emphasis will shift towards building lifelong learning models that equip students with the skills they need to navigate uncertain futures, nurture mental well-being and make a social impact.

THE FINAL HUMAN ECONOMY

By some coincidence, AI's revolution has come at the same time that we need more human-centred services. The world is hungrier than ever for healing and wellness, whether through advice or physical treatments. People who have dropped out of religion are searching for community, and mental health has become the challenge of our era. That said, traditional healthcare systems and traditional sources of wisdom are no longer popular; people feel either betrayed or unsupported by them. This means two things: the billions already spent on these industries will now move to new industries, and as more people become sick and even more seek to take preventive measures, even more billions will be going towards new kinds of solutions. We are literally at the precipice of a multi-trillion-dollar health, wellness and spiritual revolution. The best part is that, while AI will definitely be a player in this game, people will generally want help from other real people. This new movement will be about more than the provision of knowledge or intellect to solve your problems: it will be about emotional, physical and spiritual connection. On that basis alone, the demand for humans will be great. Here are four vast new emerging areas for your next role in the final human economy.

Community and collective healing

As isolation and loneliness increase, people will seek connection and shared experiences. Communities that foster collective healing will become essential. Spiritual retreats, intentional living spaces and healing circles will flourish, and practices such as dialogue, ceremonies and rituals will become an integral part of these. This shift emphasizes collective wellbeing over individual achievements to balance technology with human connection.

Alternative healthcare and wellness

The healthcare sector will expand beyond reactive treatment towards holistic wellbeing. Careers in mental health support, wellness coaching and personalized care will grow. The emphasis will shift to preventive care and to ensuring that patients receive empathetic and customized treatment plans. Relationships between healthcare providers and clients will also be intentionally crafted and tailored, with professionals fostering trust and human connection to enhance healing.

Meditation and mindfulness

As mental health challenges increase, practices such as meditation, breathwork and mindfulness will become mainstream. New roles will emerge that encompass guiding individuals and communities through these practices. This shift reflects the need to address stress, anxiety and emotional challenges with more than pharmaceutical solutions to create sustainable habits for mental wellbeing.

Therapeutic professions and emotional support services

As traditional therapy evolves, new roles will develop that blend emotional, psychological and spiritual support. Counsellors, life coaches and therapists will work on long-term wellbeing rather than short-term interventions, using both in-person and virtual sessions. Emotional intelligence, empathy and relational skills will now become more valuable than ever. This is the start of a most exciting future, where we finally have time to focus on what truly matters: human connection and evolution.

LIMITATIONS OF AI IN THE NEAR TERM

Elon Musk states that if we do not reach AGI, it will not be because of a lack of computing ability or human genius, but rather because of a shortage of energy. So while all the scenarios I have presented here are largely predictable over a 10-year timeline, what might radically increase that timeline to 15 or 20 years are some other factors that are less predictable. In some ways, this provides relief that computers won't usurp humans overnight and that we can give ourselves enough time to prepare and upskill and develop new visions for ourselves. It also gives governments enough time to develop policies for a new world running on AI, as well as an opportunity to actually understand AI first before they attempt to govern it. However, it also slows down all the exciting premises of AI. Either way, here is an overview of some possible barriers to immediate AGI or sudden technological transformations in society.

This is the story in a nutshell: To become as smart as humans, computers have to do trillions of calculations. They basically have to be able to predict all the ways in which information can come together – all the permutations and combinations of questions and answers we might have about the universe and how it works. That's a lot of work, and it can take a lot of time. But capitalism is the machine that makes progress happen much faster than without it. Larry Ellison of Oracle, Jensen Huang of Nvidia, Larry Page of Google, Elon Musk of Grok and Sam Altman of OpenAI are all effectively in a race to get to AGI first. This means they need their computers to do these calculations really quickly. To speed up their computing, they need to have faster processors. A processor such as a CPU (central processing unit) or a GPU (graphics processing unit) is a chip inside everyone's laptop or phone. The faster your laptop is, the more expensive it is. That is why there are eight different MacBooks and iPhones that you can buy at any given time. At the end of the day they all have the same software and apps and tools (at most they'll have a slightly better camera from one to another) – but you are basically paying for a faster processor so that you can run more apps at a time.

So imagine that if a top-of-the-range MacBook can run 100 apps at once and costs $5 000 dollars, then a computer that needs to manage the equivalent of one billion apps at once at top speed every single day to train data to create AGI will probably cost

$100 billion. That is what Larry Ellison, co-founder of Oracle, meant when he said, 'you need $100 billion to just enter this race'. These companies have built supercomputers that literally span acres, with millions of interconnected chips, pulling data from thousands of servers – that is why they are called 'GPU farms'. But the story doesn't end there. Mark Zuckerberg pointed out that we don't even have enough electricity supply on earth to power these massive computers and their chips. It takes a lot of power to keep these chips running all day and it takes a lot of power to cool them down, because, like a car engine running all day, they can get very hot. This is why all the software billionaires are thinking about how to harness the energy of the sun or nuclear energy to create new power sources, in order to create AI.

The intelligence level of AI that each person or company can have access to at any given time is directly correlated with how expensive it is to provide that level of AI. OpenAI literally has each ChatGPT search down to a cost per search – and on more complex or better reasoning models, the cost per search is higher than on less intelligent models, which is prompting OpenAI to charge a subscription for these services. What this indicates is that even when we reach AGI, it still might be too expensive for every company to use the tools to run their entire companies, in the early days. Sure, the cost of tech does plummet very quickly from one year to the next, but this is yet another indication that the AI revolution will not happen all at once.

MENTAL MODELS

- **The predictable AI path**: Where jobs have more predictable outcomes than others, AI is most likely to replace humans. Where job outcomes are more nuanced and case sensitive, AI is less likely to replace humans.
- Humans will be best equipped for the AI future by ranking their job tasks in order from most routine to least routine and focusing on developing broader and deeper skills related to task areas that are least routine.
- **Next job opportunities**: There is an incredible amount of opportunity in the world of new jobs and careers. These may be found in the next version of current roles in sales or marketing or design, new roles from the AI revolution such as AI ethics and robotics engineering, new problems that we need to solve, such as climate change and hunger, and new human-centred businesses, including holistic wellbeing treatments and meditation workshops.
- **Limitations of AI, for now**: Not everything in this AI future will be linear. There are some other less predictable variables that could slow down the AI revolution and buy us time as we upskill and prepare for a new future. Some of these variables are supply of energy, supply of GPUs and cost accessibility to end users. Alongside government regulation, society readiness and consumer appetite, there are at least a few hoops to jump through before AI becomes commonplace.

9

WHAT SKILLS DO
I NEED TO LEARN?

Mark Zuckerberg said that 'the best way to predict the future is to create it'. Most of us have become mindless consumers in society, eating up daily snippets of social media that instil fear in us, watching endless TV that numbs our intelligence and working lifelong jobs that slowly kill us. We don't learn to stop and think that the world and the future and the economy are not just something that is happening to us, but something created by us. People like you and me are deciding every single day what the world should be like, and the rest of us are just jumping on the train. But in the emerging future, you might have to expand your understanding of the world to succeed in it. You cannot count on your job or boss or pay cheque to write the story of a predictable life; rather, you have to be ready for change – constantly. Now you need to move from consumer to producer, viewer to creator, passive employee to entrepreneur. It is true that a great future awaits us all, one where we do not have to work and think and plan because AI does it all. But there is a road between that future and where we are now. And ironically, it is on that road that you may be required to use your brain more than you needed to in the past. This is not a scary affair – it is an exciting opportunity to reinvent yourself. And the good news is that everyone can.

This is not about working longer or harder but rather smarter and broader. Learn how the world works, get curious about how your role will evolve and recognize that, as Daniel Pink, a US-based author of a range of bestselling books about business, work, creativity and behaviour, says, 'to sell is human'. We are all selling to each other all day long. Whether you are an artist or designer or engineer or marketer – we are all in the business of selling. We are selling our products, we are selling our value in relationships, we are selling ourselves to employers and we are selling our ideas to friends. So as the world evolves, we will simply need to learn how to sell ourselves in new ways. To do that, we will need to understand the new versions of ourselves. In the previous chapter we looked at a logical framework for how your role might evolve in the AI future, but also at what opportunities might be available for you next. Now we look at the skills associated with that journey. This is the journey in a nutshell, which may not necessarily be pursued in a linear way or be exactly applicable to every person, but it will give you a useful way to think about things. It might also be wise to open your mind to the opportunities further down the path sooner, so you can craft your career accordingly.

- **Level 1 – the best version of your current job:** As AI eats up the routine tasks in your job, you will double down on the strategic and creative areas of the role. Some roles, such as customer service, in some companies, will be fully eaten up. But other roles, such as sales, will only be partially eaten up, leaving salespeople to spend time talking to more customers and building more relationships. So if 30% of your sales role is automated, then that 30% can easily be filled with more of the other tasks you are already doing.

- **Level 2 – the next version of your current job**: This is a natural extension of your role, which could happen concurrently with the above or after it. In sales you might open up new products to sell in new markets. In graphic design, you might spend more time exploring new brands for new products. In software design you might explore new solutions that can be easily integrated with or leverage existing solutions. What's happening here is that we see more innovation in each role versus expansion of current human activities.

- **Level 3 – the moonshot version of your current job**: This is where we start to get a lot more free time to think even bigger than we did in the previous step. Our companies might be doing so well as a result of innovations that we are now invited to use new, larger profits to completely reimagine futures. If you are a publisher, you might be invited to reinvent the author and reader experience. Or if you are a banker, then you might get to create a new cryptocurrency. This is where AI is taking care of a lot of our current tasks really well, assisting us in our innovative and strategic work and giving us the chance to reinvent the world.

- **Level 4 – your next job**: If the above does not happen or if your company can't think that far ahead or if you just want to do something new and cool, then those SDG industries or big problem-solving opportunities could become your next job. Millions of people will be needed to rethink and develop new systems of living, climate change economics, poverty reduction, new food and farming systems, the provision of clean water, next versions of education, and new corporate structures. This is where we move into the abundance of capital availability and innovative thinking, where money will be looking for talent to solve the next biggest issues on earth.

- **Your role in the last human economy:** While it might not be natural for this to be the final point in everyone's journey, it is certainly a possibility. Every human is interested in connecting, growing and learning. So all you need to do is find out how you want to share or what you have to give in this economy and there will always be an opportunity for you.

This is the exciting journey that will be available to all humans; it is only a matter of how prepared you will be to enjoy the fruits of the future and the abundance of these next opportunities. But if you've been in the same job for 20 years and you're thinking, 'How am I going to reinvent myself now for all of this? It's impossible for me!', just remember that there is some kid at home who knows nothing about anything and will spend the next four years learning something new to secure a job in a new world. Essentially, you have time. But you also have existing knowledge and industry experience and connections. Use what you already have, learn forever and embrace what's next.

SKILLS FOR THE NEXT VERSION OF YOUR CURRENT JOB

As AI automates roles, the most logical thing anyone can do is to investigate what new tasks they can do in their free time and then analyse what skills would be needed for these new tasks. It is also likely that you already have some of these skills to perform your job right now, but the next big questions are how you can improve those skills, what new things you should learn and what will be needed next based on how markets are evolving. For example, you might be good at building relationships to make a sale, and in 2025 that might mean you are good at winning relationships through superfluous flattery. But by 2030 great sales practice might be more about radical honesty, even if it feels scary. Podcasts are getting bigger because people are becoming increasingly sceptical about traditional news channels and they are yearning for authenticity. Even in social media, those who show up as themselves are rewarded most. We are now in an era where people want to see things exactly as they are, not some polished version of it. So it is natural that we will see more of this across other human relationships and contexts. These are the nuances we need to pay attention to next as we maximize our existing uniquely human skill sets.

To illustrate a new way of looking at your old job, the table that follows expands on the three roles discussed in the previous chapter. Again, I used ChatGPT to create the table, which at first might seem super basic, but this approach is truly useful for training your mind to formulate a logical upskilling plan for yourself, based on your role. The ability to break down your thinking into a framework such as this gives you a plan for your future career and virtually eliminates the fear of AI creeping into your industry. You can simply enter your role or job into ChatGPT and ask it to show you these columns. ChatGPT is quite good at giving you some foundational answers, but then you will need to apply your own industry insights to these answers to figure out what really applies to you. Here is how the table is structured:

- As AI does more routine tasks for you and you get more free time, you can start doubling down on a new set of responsibilities to provide value in your role. For each of the three roles below, you can see these new responsibilities emerging in the second column. It could also be useful to have a conversation with your manager or friends in the industry to better predict what these new tasks will be.

- In the third column we ask ChatGPT to show us the key skills that we will need so as to perform the tasks in the previous column. The ability to identify and distil these skills into one or two points will reduce overwhelm and give you a focus. Much of what you really need to know is simply a minor upgrade of what you already know. A few hours a month should suffice in helping you get to the next version of you, and being specific about what the next version of you entails will increase the chances of you getting there.
- In the final two columns I attempt to get ultra-clear on what it would actually be like to use that skill in a new context, as well as how to learn that skill. You might think you know what it means to improve your 'critical thinking' or better your 'interpersonal communication' because these words are so generic and ubiquitous, but getting clarity by finding an example of that skill in action, and being specific or intentional about how to learn it, will vastly increase your chances of learning the best version of that skill and being able to use it in the AI era.

MOONSHOTS AND SDGS

Now we are going to do something rather interesting. Let's imagine that at some point such a large percentage of your work is automated that you are only required to be at work for 1.5 days a week to do strategic or creative work in your current role. This would free up time for you to work on moonshots or other big global problems, such as those mentioned in the previous chapter. But which is best for you to work on and how do you imagine the leap from being an accountant to solving climate change challenges or from being a teacher to ending world hunger? The answer is simple: you will need to know which of your skills are

Role	New tasks to focus on as AI does routine work	Key skills to maximize return	Example of skill in action	How to learn the skill
Lawyer	Build deeper client relationships, engage in complex case preparation	Critical thinking	Identifying complex legal issues in cases and developing innovative strategies	Join case study analysis workshops, practise with logic puzzles or mock trials
		Interpersonal communication	Presenting complicated legal information in clear terms to clients	Take public-speaking courses, join debate clubs or enrol in negotiation-training programmes
Professor	Focus on advanced research, student mentorship and innovative teaching methods	Innovation	Designing new course materials and research methodologies	Join innovation seminars, experiment with creative teaching methods and attend conferences
		Analytical thinking	Analysing student performance data to improve teaching outcomes	Engage in statistical and data interpretation training, take education-focused data analysis courses
Doctor	Engage in patient wellness initiatives and mentor medical staff	Empathy	Comforting patients during difficult diagnoses	Attend workshops on empathy in healthcare and wellbeing, engage in role-play exercises focused on patient interaction
		Advanced medical knowledge	Utilizing cutting-edge treatment techniques	Engage in continuing medical education, attend medical conferences and complete advanced certifications

transferable, but also which new skill sets are easiest for you to learn. You can, of course, also completely reinvent yourself, but life is busy and sometimes it is easier to leap into something closer to where you are.

In the next table we look at the SDG problem areas where we know many new opportunities will be. As an example, let's look at how the skills in some of the roles mentioned earlier can be applied to these new problems. The third column mentions the specific transferable skills that will help someone in these new industries. What we notice is that there is actually immense opportunity available to us when we can simply recontextualize our skill sets to reposition ourselves for newer environments, which will make us valuable all over again. This implies that our understanding of our skill sets and our ability to communicate them in different contexts is what keeps us marketable and relevant in a new world. There is great value in simply sitting down and asking yourself, 'What have I learnt?' and 'What skills do I have and how can I apply them in other areas?'

In the fourth column we find a list of the skills or knowledge areas we could add on to our existing skill sets. This column is insightful because it shows us that if you simply take an extra course in something related to a new industry, all of sudden you seem like a 'perfect fit'. So if you are an accountant who wants to work in climate change, you might at first be perceived as an accountant who has lost their way. But if you take a six-week course at Stanford University on carbon accounting, all of a sudden you become this great accountant from PwC who specializes in carbon accounting methods. Now you look useful to a new firm in this space *and* you have learnt how to apply yourself differently – and the leap between where you are now and where you once were was not even that huge.

SDG problem	Role and example	Transferable skills	New skills to learn
SDG 2: Zero hunger – sustainable agriculture	**Consultant** Consultants can apply strategic planning and supply chain optimization to address food security challenges and support sustainable food systems with their understanding of agricultural policy and practices	**Strategic planning**: Skilled in developing scalable strategies, key for designing sustainable food systems **Stakeholder communication**: Experienced in liaising across sectors for effective implementation **Supply chain optimization**: Expertise in improving supply chains, which is essential for reducing food waste and improving distribution	Agricultural systems and policy knowledge
SDG 3: Good health and wellbeing – access to mental health support	**HR specialist** HR professionals with experience in employee wellness programmes can extend support to community-wide mental health solutions, emphasizing confidentiality and trauma-informed practices	**Employee support programmes**: Familiar with wellness initiatives, transferable to broader mental health programmes **Confidentiality and ethical sensitivity**: Essential in mental health for building trust **Crisis management**: Experience in conflict resolution, useful for responsive mental health services	Public-health and trauma-informed practices
SDG 4: Quality education – bridging the digital divide	**Teacher** Teachers can leverage their adaptability and empathy to provide inclusive digital education in underserved communities to help reduce the digital divide and enhance personalized learning	**Adaptability and personalization**: Skilled at tailoring approaches for diverse learners, which is crucial for creating inclusive education **Empathy and cultural awareness**: Ability to connect across different backgrounds to support equitable education **Digital fluency**: Familiar with educational technologies to enhance students' digital access and learning	Inclusive pedagogies and tech access solutions

SDG problem	Role and example	Transferable skills	New skills to learn
SDG 11: Sustainable cities – urban planning	**Designer** Designers experienced in ergonomic and environmental design can innovate in sustainable urban spaces, focusing on human-centred design and eco-friendly solutions	**Human-centred design**: Expertise in user experience and ergonomics, helpful for sustainable urban spaces **Creative problem solving**: Brings innovation to urban design, focused on green solutions **Environmental awareness**: Experience in evaluating environmental impact, crucial for sustainable city planning	Urban planning and social equity principles
SDG 13: Climate action – carbon emission reduction	**Accountant** Accountants with strong regulatory knowledge and financial analysis skills can guide firms in transitioning to carbon-neutral practices by incorporating carbon accounting and sustainability reporting	**Financial analysis for sustainability**: Skilled in evaluating costs, essential for calculating and reducing carbon footprints **Compliance and regulatory knowledge**: Familiar with adherence to standards, guiding businesses in carbon compliance **Data analysis**: Capable of working with large datasets, enabling efficient tracking of emission goals	Environmental economics and carbon accounting

WHAT IS GREAT STRATEGIC THINKING?

As we accept that AI is there for routine tasks and that we will be applying ourselves to more strategic and creative thinking, it will be wise to get clear about what that actually means. You can't acquire this thinking by reading a book about it or hope to inadvertently master it from your everyday work. You have to also reflect on the bigger picture – all the adjacent abilities, styles of thought and topics that support world-class strategy and creativity. It would also be beneficial to research different styles of problem solving, because that is effectively the purpose of strategy and creativity in business, and see how thinkers from different disciplines approach a particular topic. You want to build a toolbox of problem-solving abilities that you can draw from at any time, to become indispensable. You'll also want to develop wider knowledge beyond your immediate work needs and develop an understanding of topics such as science, business, technology and sociology to have a better grasp of the world. But to make things easy, let's look at some good basic fields of knowledge about which everyone should know more.

- **Psychology**: Steve Jobs made it clear that technology is always applied to humans and humans can only be learnt about in the humanities – and it is Apple's understanding of humans that has helped it build a great company. Psychology is only one subject in the humanities, but we need to begin with an understanding of how humans think and behave; then all good things flow from there. This is probably why American universities make everyone, including doctors and scientists, take a liberal arts foundation for two years. We need to learn about sociology, anthropology, psychology, philosophy and history to get a sense of what it means to be a human being and how we came to our beliefs and behaviours, or how we perceive ourselves and our relationship with the world around us. Until now, business psychology has mainly been used as a tool to manipulate people, but the general public is becoming increasingly aware of this, so the next natural use of business psychology is to see how we can enlighten people. This is more important than ever in an AI age where deeper understanding of human nature will exponentially increase possibilities for us.

- **Business**: The whole world is a business, so if you under-stand that and know how to build a business you will always be able to see opportunity. People make business more complicated than it is, while it is really just making, selling, and coordinating making and selling. When you can see business as simply as this, you can start to expand your thinking in each. Making includes areas such as product design, manufacturing and prototyping. Selling includes areas such as marketing, sales and partnership development. And coordinating includes operations, project management and finance. You might believe that you are merely an engineer and that sales is not for you, or that you are only a marketing person and that design is not your area of expertise. But while that is true to some degree, in the AI age we all need to know how to create opportunity, so it is important to understand a little bit about how the world of business works and take an interest in it. If you won't be a business owner (it's certainly not necessary for everyone), at least you can think like one – and if you can think like one, then at least you can always find one to work for.

- **First principles thinking**: Business is effectively problem solving – if you solve a problem for me, I will pay you a fee for it – and so all day long we are simply solving problems for each other. But the best way to be a great problem solver is to learn first principles thinking. First principles thinking involves breaking down complex problems to their most basic, foundational elements and then rebuilding them from the ground up. This scientific approach enables innovative thinking by allowing us to challenge assumptions and completely reimagine the future. But it's not a complicated method only available to smart people; children are all born as great first principles thinkers; they come into a world they know nothing about and question everything about it. 'Mommy, why does the light go on when you press the switch? But why does electricity come into the light bulb? But why does electricity come from the power station? But why does coal create electricity?' Children are naturally curious about how things work, and as adults we naturally accept that things just work a certain way. Of course, things don't simply 'work' a certain way; someone like you and me decided that they do. We can change that and reinvent the way things work. The child who asks how we get light could be the adult who creates a renewable energy source. When we go back to basics, this leads us to new questions and solutions.

- **Systems thinking**: The world is merely a group of systems with people, activities and decisions. If you understand the main systems and how they connect, then you can be very adaptable. Systems thinking is about seeing the big picture and understanding that different areas such as business, economics, design, culture and politics are all connected. For example, if five Fortune 100 companies adopt a new billion-dollar AI technology, this has a major impact on their efficiency and also influences the job market (economics), changes customer expectations (culture) and may lead to new regulations (politics). Moreover, this new AI technology can improve customer experience and make all these companies more competitive, which could in turn drive economic growth and inspire cultural trends. Systems thinking helps people look beyond isolated pockets of global activity and actually see how these areas interact with each other. So, as AI shapes the future, your constant quest to discover how different areas connect to and influence each other will exponentially increase your chances of effectively navigating a new world. This is not so much something you need to 'seek out': by simply paying attention to the world, conversations, people's feelings and different sources of information and combining these observations with your own inner voice, you'll find great clarity about the interconnected nature of things.

- **Intuitive thinking:** In our age of knowledge abundance, discernment is key. And in a context of a plethora of great AI-produced solutions, backed by solid logical, scientific and critical thinking, discernment can only come from intuition. For instance, understanding consumer needs in emerging markets often involves a level of cultural and emotional or seemingly illogical insight that AI lacks. When you are presented with what AI thinks is the best way forward, you need to start moving from thinking to feeling. Most smart people think they run everything on logic, but, as Jeff Bezos says, 'we often only have 70% of the data to make a decision'. We never have 100% of all available data, so let's just work with what we have. In other words, science and critical thought can bring us to a certain point of clarity, but intuition is often what is used to make the final leap. Intuitive thinking is about developing trust in oneself and the process, knowing that what you might 'feel' you need to do in any given situation is the best solution, and then simply iterating or improving the outcomes as new information presents itself.

Finally, you will find it useful to become a brilliant T-thinker. This means developing deep thought in one or two disciplines and having a breadth of knowledge across all disciplines (the horizontal line of the letter T represents breadth and the vertical line represents depth). Some of the world's best thinkers have this ability, which is why they seem able to do almost anything. This means you could be an actor, an engineer or a salesperson at the highest level, but no matter which of these you are, you will have knowledge about business, science, design, culture, economics and politics. This breadth of knowledge is what enables you to be so good at what you do in your niche, because it provides perspective. This is why many strategy professors at the world's leading business schools will say that you cannot learn much about strategy in a 14-week semester course. The ability to strategize comes from life experience, exposure to the workings of the world and interest in life itself – and using all of this to develop unique insights to build great companies and products.

Elon Musk is a T-thinker, but also what we might call a 'triple threat' – another useful concept. What this means is that he has deep thinking skills across strategy, design and engineering. Someone who is a triple threat can imagine the creation of anything (based on sound design principles), can build whatever they imagined (based on solid engineering principles) and can sell what they built (based on solid strategic and business thinking). Google X, which solves Google's most ambitious problems, is known to hire triple threats because they can pretty much do everything on their own in the early stages of inventing something. It is also incredibly useful for a CEO of any company building and influencing the future to be a triple threat, because such people know how to hire and manage anyone in their business, product and operations departments. As a T-thinker, you become someone who understands everyone, which provides you with the opportunity to create world-class cohesion between teams to achieve unimaginable feats. And even if you cannot be great at all three of these areas, it is important to develop some depth of understanding in each, as this will exponentially increase your chances of being forever relevant in a new world, no matter your role or expertise.

MENTAL MODELS

- **Your next five jobs**: You can envision your future through these next five roles: the best version of your current job (getting to spend more time on strategic and creative tasks, as AI takes up routine tasks); the next version of your current job (expanding into new markets, developing new ideas and building new products related to your current job); the moonshot version of your current job (reimagining what your department or company will look like in a new future and designing your next natural role within that); your next job (focusing on SDGs and areas of need in the world where capital will flow to next); and your role in the last human economy (recognizing the trillion-dollar wellness, wellbeing, community-oriented and alternative health industries that will be largely human-centred and require many different thinkers).

- **ChatGPT your next role**: Just as I did for the five roles in the first point, you can use ChatGPT to develop a comprehensive learning plan. Simply enter your role into it, for example 'I am a salesperson at a publishing house' or 'I am a designer at a marketing agency' (the more specific your wording, the better, so include the name of your firm and your country of operation too), and then ask it to produce a table under these headings: Identify new tasks to focus on as AI does routine work in my role in column 1; identify the key skills I need to maximize my return in column 2; show me an example of these new skills in action in column 3; and show me how to learn the skill in column 4. You will need to do deeper research too, but this will train you to think about maintaining your relevance in the future. You can learn more on how to use

ChatGPT in 'Your guide to getting started with AI' at the end of this book.

- **Great strategic thinking:** Strategy and creativity cannot be learnt in a single book about these topics; instead, you will need to develop broader thinking skills in areas such as psychology for human motivation, the basics of business to launch and manage ventures, first principles thinking for great problem solving, systems thinking to see how the world's activities are connected, intuitive thinking to discern between various sound logical paths, and T-thinking to understand the world more broadly and apply broad thinking to your area of expertise.

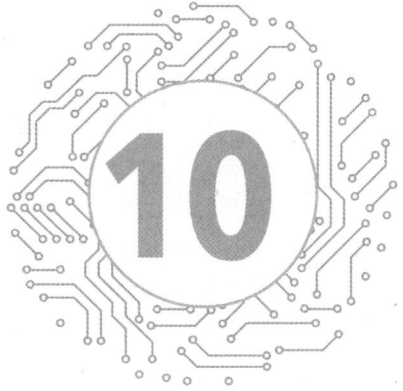

KEY FUTURE MINDSETS

In 2014, Carol Dweck, a professor at Stanford University, delivered a TED Talk on the power of believing in a growth mindset. It has since been viewed millions of times and has become the foundational philosophy in beginning what schools now call 'mindsets training'. In this talk, she discusses how our mindset shapes the way we approach challenges and setbacks, and she emphasizes that adopting a growth mindset can radically change our approach to learning, resilience and achievement. Here are the two main mindsets:

- **Fixed mindset**: People with a fixed mindset believe their abilities and intelligence are set traits that can't change. They tend to avoid challenges, give up easily and view effort as pointless if they're not naturally 'good' at something.
- **Growth mindset**: People with a growth mindset believe their abilities can be developed through effort, learning and persistence. They embrace challenges, learn from criticism and see failure as an opportunity to grow.

Her work brings practicality to the age-old philosophy that 'when you change the way you look at things, the things you look at change'. This means that mindsets are not about tricking your brain into only seeing the good in things, but rather about actively shaping the world in a direction that is consistent with your thoughts – because there are unlimited options and the ones we focus on are the ones we materialize. The world is like clay; it has plentiful resources in the ground and abundant energy from the sun, so it is malleable and can be shaped into all the beautiful experiences we want to have. Basic economics proves this to be true and social media is beginning to show us the brighter side of life on earth that traditional news networks typically never shared.

What humanity is now realizing is that it is not so much that opportunities are scarce, but rather that if you believe opportunities are scarce then you will most likely find yourself fighting in markets with little space. But if you believe opportunities are endless, you will start to see markets where there is almost no competition. From an objective standpoint – there is no mystery to this – there are simply highly competitive markets and highly underserved markets. If you search more for the latter, then you will most likely find them. You are literally training your eye to see differently – and that's the magic of mindsets.

But a 'growth mindset' is just one of the mindsets that has been widely popularized. There are others too, and smart people use them every day to navigate business and life decisions. In the AI era, this training is particularly valuable, because it helps people see opportunities rather than obstacles in a world that will be increasingly shaped by automation. Let's consider three mindsets that are beneficial in the AI era.

The abundance mindset – 'life is abundant'

The abundance mindset is rooted in the belief that the world offers endless opportunities, especially as technology advances. With AI's capacity to scale production, design new services and enhance efficiency, adopting an abundance perspective means believing that there is enough room for everyone to create, succeed and grow. This can also be a powerful motivator to pursue ambitious projects or jobs without fearing scarcity or competition. In some ways this can look just like a way of thinking, but it is actually a reality that has been economically and scientifically proven. In a world built on scarcity thinking, we could be easily swayed towards a negative mindset instead of a positive one – which is why training an abundance mindset is now more useful than ever.

The prosperity mindset – 'everyone can be rich'

Inspired by entrepreneur and investor Naval Ravikant's philosophy, the prosperity mindset is about recognizing that wealth is not a zero-sum game – meaning that just because my neighbour is getting rich, this doesn't mean that I cannot be rich too, or just because you win it doesn't mean that I have to lose. This mindset encourages people to pursue personal wealth by making use of the tools at their disposal – be it through building businesses, upskilling or investing in emerging fields. By seeing AI as an enabler, people can approach their goals knowing that the potential for wealth generation is accessible to everyone willing to make it happen.

The meaningful existence mindset – 'humans are not meant for routine work'

The meaningful existence mindset reminds us that people are inherently better suited for complex and meaningful tasks as opposed to repetitive ones. An anti-routine mindset allows people to see the rise of AI as an opportunity to elevate their careers as they focus on where humans uniquely fit into newer versions of work versus fighting every chance to hold on to their current jobs. With this mindset you learn about new technologies, you get excited to read about AI developments, and you keep stretching your mind to find out how you can add value to newer societies and economies. In the previous chapter we looked at your 'next five jobs'. If you hold on to a fear-oriented mindset, you might hold on to each job with all your strength before being forced into your next job. A 'meaningful existence mindset', by contrast, immediately allows you to become excited to learn about what you can do next.

DEEPER INNER MINDSETS

From one angle you might feel like 'you do not *have* enough', and that is what the three mindsets in the previous section address, while from another angle you might feel like 'you *are* not enough'. The latter is often deeply unconscious in ways that can severely limit what you can achieve in life. When you become aware of these unconscious beliefs and turn them into new useful mind-sets, this can be utterly life-changing. In a period of great change, during which we need to access new sources of human potential, managing your inner chatter will become a priceless skill. The influential psychologist Abraham Maslow studied this in a very organized way when he looked at the 'psychology of motivation'. One of his great frameworks is his hierarchy of needs, which every student studies at least once in high school. This hierarchy is simple: it is organized from our most critical human needs to our more aspirational needs – all the way from food and shelter at the bottom to belonging and self-esteem at the top – with the general understanding that as humans fulfil their lower-order needs, more of their attention can go towards fulfilling their higher-order needs. That's the general public understanding in a nutshell.

But what is less well known is that Maslow divided the hierarchy of needs into two sections, which he called *deficiency needs* and *growth needs*. The lower part of the hierarchy is what he called physiological deficiencies – food, shelter and physical security – and the higher part of the hierarchy he called psychological deficiencies – all the needs associated with belonging, self-esteem, respect and achievement, with the exception of self-actualization, the pinnacle of the hierarchy, which he called growth needs.

His theory is that you are motivated towards pursuing psychological deficiency needs because you never 'feel good enough'. But when you become self-actualized, you came from a place of growth – 'feeling enough and complete' – yet wanting to grow into the best version of yourself. This was an important distinction, because it helped people understand that most humans live in such a way that they do not feel they are good enough. With the exception of pursuing food and shelter, which is key to basic mammalian survival, most humans spend the majority of their existence and mental energy pursuing respect, status, achievement, belonging and recognition. It is as though we are slaves to our never-ending need for self-validation.

But those who truly self-actualized (Einstein, Gandhi and Viktor Frankl, as Maslow pointed out) were in fact in a state of feeling absolutely complete. They did not pursue their work for fame and fortune, or for respect and achievement. It is perhaps for that reason that they were able to achieve so much. They were not like a pendulum, swinging between feeling loved and unloved, using the frivolous nature of these feelings to validate their life's work. They were simply in pursuit of growing into the best versions of themselves, while moving humanity forward. And so, according to Maslow, this is the natural trajectory for human motivation, that humans might eventually realize their best selves if they contemplate the leap from being slaves to their deficiencies to accepting the completeness within themselves.

But to get more practical, psychological deficiencies are merely deficiencies or needs of the mind, not of the body. And since we know that we can alter the way we think, we know that we can virtually eliminate the need for those hardwired goals. For example, you do not need respect from others – it is merely something you think you need to navigate reality. Also, respect is not something you can really acquire anyway; it is only something you think you can. You believe that someone sees you in a certain way, and therefore treats you in a certain way, so you 'feel respected'. But they may not actually respect you at all. Mostly, no one says outright, 'I respect you' – respect is generally assumed. So it could be that this person simply treats you well to get something from you or to behave politely towards you. By contrast, if someone treats you 'badly', you might think they do not respect you. But a wiser person might conclude that others' interactions are never personal, because each person lives in their own mental dream, as Don Miguel Ruiz, famous author of *The Four Agreements*, says, and never does anything because of you but because of them. So it might not be that they disrespect you as much as they are having a rough day or simply showing you their raw emotions. The same applies to all the other perceived psychological needs that we spend so much of our time and lives pursuing: esteem, achievement and recognition. It is like an empty pit that can never be filled, and the only reason these needs are pursued is because we never feel enough.

It can be useful to become clear about our deeper deficiency-oriented beliefs, especially in the AI age, which requires us to be well prepared to navigate uncertain territory and tap into all our unique human skills. Once you stop chasing these elusive needs, you free up a lot of mental space to see the world more clearly. This is precisely what machines do not struggle with and therefore one reason why their processing power is so much more powerful than ours. They are seeing things objectively instead of pursuing empty status needs or wasting mental energy playing emotional games. Moreover, as Elon Musk alluded to, machines do not design their lives to have the most amount of sex – which can be fun and completely natural in moderation, but is also effectively a dopamine chase and a 'senseless' human act without the goal of reproduction when pursued consistently. Intimacy, connection and love are beautiful, but when we live in such a way as to dedicate all our cortex power to feeding the needs of the limbic system, we are missing out on much larger insights in life, or on much more useful abilities. Effectively, if we look more closely at what motivates us and why we behave in certain ways, we can unlock immense human potential.

Now is the time for humans to step up in their intelligence and access all those beautiful unique human powers – and this is largely where it begins. We must start with engineering our inner worlds, as famous monks like Sadhguru and Thich Nhat Hanh say, before we can have a significant impact on our outer worlds. This is where living from a place of growth needs becomes useful. A growth-mindset way of life doesn't stem from continuously feeling a lack of something inside yourself, but rather from a desire to grow as a person. In other words, you can still enjoy connection, intimacy, status, belonging, achievement and sex – except now you no longer need them.

FIVE MANTRAS TO REWIRE YOUR MINDSET

There are many great books on the topic of the negative mindsets shared by most of humanity that dominate a large part of our conscious and unconscious thinking power. Here I wish to share five problem mindsets and the mantras you can use to counter them. It is crucial to identify your own deficiency needs, write them down and then write down the alternative mantra or mindset to begin to rewire yourself. They are called 'mantras', because you can recite them when you wake up, and they can be an extremely useful start to your day. Just like machines, we become what we constantly expose ourselves to, but we can also retrain our neural networks to respond better to outside prompts and inputs.

While science is confirming how activities such as meditation and prayer can fundamentally rewire your neural networks, some basic, logical mindset training can also help you change your neural wiring profoundly. You can delve deeply into relinquishing unhelpful needs by exploring why you feel the way you do and why these feelings are unnecessary. A good way to do this is through daily journalling or therapy, which will enable you to see that all your problems have the same root cause: 'I do not feel I am enough' or 'I do not feel good enough about myself'. When you use therapy or journalling as a space to identify the root causes of your deeper feelings, you open the door to immense power to deal with the future. For now, I offer five new mantras to train your mindset for the AI future:

- 'I am not good enough.'
  - 'I have nothing more to prove to the world.'
- 'I don't deserve this.'
  - 'Life is to be enjoyed, and I deserve to enjoy life.'
- 'They might think I am dumb.'
  - 'Nothing is ever personal; I am free to try new things.'
- 'I'm running out of time in life to achieve my goals.'
  - 'The next opportunity is just around the corner.'
- 'I'm not sure they like me.'
  - 'There are people out there who resonate perfectly with me.'

PLURAL FUTURE MINDSETS

There is no such thing as 'the future', or the one and only future, and as I move towards the end of this book I want to share a post I saw on LinkedIn that spoke to this mindset. It was written by Enrica Beccalli, a Fulbright scholar from Parsons School of Design and UX designer for a large technology company in New York. She is a native Italian speaker, with English as her second language, but because of this her written English comes across as more raw and real. As I wrote this book and used ChatGPT to help describe some complex concepts in it, I became aware of the difference between what computer and human writing feels like. The words may be the same, but there is a distinct difference between how they feel, depending on who produced a text. Perhaps, once AI can produce any type of written work, we will all become more aware of the feeling behind words – as though we can tell whether a person's soul was poured into that text or not. In an overly curated world with perfectly crafted messages about the future, that is what I felt when I read Beccalli's piece – she was offering a raw piece of her soul with a deeper message for humanity.

She seemed to describe the current era in such a beautiful way that the only logical thing to do was use her piece in this book instead of attempting to rewrite it. When I gave her a call to ask her if this was fine, we ended up having a long conversation about how language is such a strong indicator of truth. It is as though we choose words and definitions that truly capture the real meanings of things and so, if we want to contemplate higher truths, there is also much to learn from simply reading the dictionary or studying the Latin origins of our speech. She was also the one who told me that 'humanitas' is the Latin word for humanity, which is also a synonym for the word compassion. She helped me to see that humanity can be summed up as compassion, and that anything we really need to know about being human lies in that one word – a word upon which an entire book series can be written and upon which an entirely new society can be developed. This is probably because we understand so little about it – so little about what it means in practice and how it can be used as a foundational value for developing the future: compassion for oneself, for one's neighbour, for the natural environment and for the world at large. This is the future in which we will ask these higher-order questions, because, in essence, compassion is *what humans are really for in the AI age*. But for now, let me simply end with Beccalli's piece.

As we say in Rome, 'nessuno ci obbliga a farlo diventare così' (no one is forcing us to make it this way). Out of the myriad possible futures, we don't have to accept one that looks like a tech dystopia filled with flying cars, robots controlled by Elon Musk, and Neuralink-powered hyper-humans.

This future – so often painted as the pinnacle of human achievement – might work for some, but for many of us, it's a deeply unattractive vision. Personally, I don't want to live in a world that feels like the cold, mechanical universe of *I, Robot*. Instead, the future I imagine is closer to Eden: one filled with nature, community, balance, and harmony. A future where technology supports human well-being rather than controlling or alienating us.

We must remind ourselves that the future is not set in stone. It's not an inevitable march towards some sterile, mechanized existence. It's a creation – a story we write. The same people who have painted it as grey and robotic are not the ones who get to define it for everyone. We have the power to build a future based on our values, and we should be deliberate about imagining futures that are beautiful, sustainable, and truly reflective of the kind of world we want to live in.

In this moment, as technology advances at a rapid pace, it's more important than ever to resist the passive acceptance of someone else's vision of the future. We should be critical and creative, always asking: is this really the world I want to live in? What alternatives are there? Because in the end, the future can be as diverse and beautiful as we choose to make it.

Since thinking about the future is an innate and constant part of our thoughts, my favourite exercise is to consciously replace the grey, lifeless image with one that is green, vibrant, and full of life.

MENTAL MODELS

- **General mindsets**: The future is more easily navigated when you have these four great mindsets: growth, abundance, prosperity and meaning. To some degree things objectively work a certain way, but to another degree we do not see things as they are but as we are. In other words, we also live in the reality we believe in. Those who believe in scarcity will fight for a share in small markets, but those who believe in abundance will start to see new markets. So change your perception – and you will change your life.
- **Inner mindsets**: Most of your psychological problems in life can be reduced to one line: 'I do not feel good about myself.' Abraham Maslow said that when we move away from our need for respect, achievement, recognition and validation, we begin to realize that we are enough. On this basis, we can begin to turn our focus towards growth needs and the joy of simply being, and experience all the beautiful things in life without needing them either. This was Maslow's theory about being motivated by deficiency

needs or growth needs – the difference between everyday humans and those who have reached a state of self-actualization.

- **Plural futures**: There is no one future and no single narrative for where we are headed, so we must not blindly heed the ideas that are being presented and marketed to us the most. We must realize that we choose our future, and that through each action we are actively doing so. Everyone has a different idea of what makes a beautiful and exciting future, so if we remain true to that we will find more people in our tribe and we will travel together towards the futures we specifically yearn for. The final outcome is one that is balanced and benefits all of society.

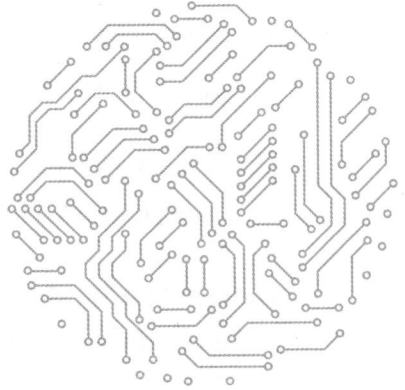

YOUR GUIDE TO GETTING STARTED WITH AI

WHERE DO I BEGIN WITH AI TODAY?

By the time this book reaches your hands, most of the world will be familiar with AI, or will have typed at least one question into ChatGPT. But in case you are only getting started now, this guide will prove useful. I used ChatGPT to draft this chapter, but I have highly tailored it to meet your needs. It is also a great guide to share with a friend or around your office with new joiners to the AI revolution. Finally, even if you already use AI or ChatGPT frequently, this section will contextualize what you already know into simple mental models that can enhance your own thinking as well as that of those around you at work and at home. Enjoy!

FOUNDATIONAL UNDERSTANDING

If you're eager to get started with AI, the good news is that you don't need a tech degree or years of experience to jump in. The landscape of AI is rich and varied, with tools and resources accessible to everyone. Here's how to begin your journey.

Understand AI basics and potential benefits

AI refers to technology that can learn, reason and make decisions, similar to the human brain. It works by using large amounts of data and algorithms (instructions) to make sense of patterns, learn from them, and make predictions or recommendations. For instance, an AI tool could analyse customer preferences in your sales data or Google Sheets to suggest better marketing strategies. At its simplest, AI handles repetitive tasks, freeing up time for more valuable work; at its most complex, it can drive insights and reveal opportunities for growth.

Start with simple tools to get comfortable

For beginners, it's best to start with AI tools that are easy to use. ChatGPT, for example, is great for drafting emails quickly, generating content ideas or outlining presentations. You can use it by typing a simple prompt, such as 'Help me create a plan for a product launch', to get ideas in seconds. Many of these tools are free or have trial versions, so you can explore them without committing to a purchase. Trying out simple tools will help you get a feel for how AI can work for you without needing technical skills or special training.

Use AI-powered project-management tools

Project-management tools such as Asana and Trello have integrated AI features that help manage your team's tasks and deadlines. These tools allow you to organize and assign work to team members and track project progress. The AI features in these tools can make suggestions, such as which team member might be best for a task, or where there are potential project delays. AI-powered project-management tools allow you to save time on task management and get a better view of your team's workload to help keep projects on track.

Focus on your specific business needs

When selecting AI tools, think about your unique challenges or about the areas where you want to improve efficiency. For example, if you spend a lot of time analysing customer data, look for AI tools that specialize in data analysis, such as **Tableau**. It can turn complex data into easy-to-read charts and graphs, enabling you to see trends and make decisions based on real insights. Or, if you spend a lot of time designing graphics, look at **Canva** with its AI tools. It can take your ideas and design slides or graphics for you with a focus on function and good aesthetics. If you struggle with repetitive tasks, automation tools can handle them, allowing you to focus on strategic work. For example, any mom-and-pop shop can use a tool such as **Landbot** to create a custom chatbot to answer customer queries on their website – no coding required. Identifying your needs will help you find the right AI tools to enhance your workflow.

Invest in learning about AI

Learning about AI will increase your confidence in using these tools and help you understand how they can influence your work. Many online courses and tutorials are available on platforms such as **Coursera** and **Udemy**. These platforms offer classes on specific topics, such as AI in marketing or data analytics, designed by experts. Taking even a basic course will give you a stronger foundation and help you stay competitive as AI becomes a bigger part of business. Start with the basics, play with random tools, and then talk to people in your industry to find out about other specific courses and tools you could take and use.

HOW DO I GET STARTED WITH CHATGPT?

The easiest and least intimidating way to get started with AI is by using ChatGPT. It's free – and intuitive. You ask questions and get answers; that's it!

Step 1: What is ChatGPT?

ChatGPT is an AI-powered tool that can answer questions, help with research, write and brainstorm ideas. It's different from Google because instead of merely finding links to information, ChatGPT actually responds to you in sentences, as in a conversation. Think of it as a helpful assistant that learns from lots of information but responds in a way that feels more interactive than a typical search engine.

Step 2: How to download ChatGPT (or use it online)

- **For app users** (on iPhone or Android):
  - Open your device's app store (for example, the Apple App Store or Google Play Store).
  - Search for 'ChatGPT' by OpenAI.
  - Download the app, open it, and sign up or log in with your email address.
- **For web users** (if you prefer a web browser):
  - Go to chat.openai.com
  - Click 'Sign up' if you're a new user or 'Log in' if you already have an account.
  - Follow the prompts to create an account using your email or a Google login.

Step 3: How to use ChatGPT

- **Start a conversation**: Simply type in your question or ask for help in the chat box. For example, you could write, 'Help me brainstorm a birthday gift for my friend.'
- **Get a response**: ChatGPT will respond in real time, giving you answers, ideas or step-by-step explanations.
- **Ask follow-up questions**: You can keep asking related questions to get more details or explanations.

How ChatGPT compares to Google

- **ChatGPT**: Gives conversational answers, insights and even creative content based on the vast data it's been trained on. It's like talking to a very knowledgeable friend.
- **Google**: Shows you links to websites that may have the information you need, and you'll usually read or explore those links yourself.

With ChatGPT, there's no need to sift through multiple websites – it provides direct responses. However, Google can still be better for finding specific articles or very recent news. Starting with ChatGPT is a great way to try out a new, interactive way of learning, researching and getting creative ideas.

HOW DO I USE AI AT WORK?

Incorporating AI into your work can feel daunting, but once you understand its applications across various departments, you'll see it's a powerful ally. Let's explore how AI can enhance productivity in four key areas: sales, marketing, human resources and finance/operations.

Sales

In sales, AI can drastically change how teams engage with prospects. For example, tools such as **Salesforce Einstein** provide predictive analytics to help sales teams prioritize leads based on their likelihood to convert. It analyses past data to suggest which leads to follow up with first, thereby saving salespeople time and increasing conversion rates.

AI can also help with drafting sales emails. Tools such as **Reply.io** utilize AI to create personalized email outreach based on the recipient's interests and behaviours. This means that, instead of spending hours crafting individual messages, sales reps can use AI-generated templates and focus more on building relationships.

Marketing

AI is a game changer in marketing too. Platforms such as **HubSpot** use AI algorithms to optimize marketing campaigns in real time. For instance, they analyse engagement data to determine the best time to send emails or which content types resonate most with particular audiences. This allows marketers to adjust their strategies instantly, rather than waiting for a campaign to finish to analyse results.

Another great example is content generation. AI writing tools such as **Jasper** or **Copy.ai** can help create blog posts, social media content and ad copy. By entering a few keywords, marketers can generate multiple drafts, reducing the time spent on brainstorming and writing.

Human resources

In HR, AI simplifies many tasks, from recruitment to employee engagement. For instance, tools such as **HireVue** use AI to screen résumés and conduct initial video interviews, assessing candidates' suitability based on their responses and body language. This speeds up the hiring process and helps identify the best candidates faster.

AI also plays a role in employee retention. Platforms such as **Glint** analyse employee feedback in real time, offering insights into engagement levels and potential issues. By identifying trends before they escalate, HR can proactively address concerns and improve workplace satisfaction.

Finance/operations

In finance and operations, AI tools such as **Adaptive Insights** enable predictive modelling and budgeting. They analyse historical financial data to project future revenues and expenses, allowing teams to make informed decisions. This reduces the time spent on manual calculations and enhances the accuracy of forecasts.

AI-driven automation tools such as **UiPath** can streamline repetitive tasks across departments. For instance, they can automate data entry, invoice processing and even customer service inquiries, freeing up employees to focus on strategic initiatives rather than mundane tasks.

WHAT TOOLS SHOULD I LEARN?

As you start exploring AI, selecting the right tools can dramatically boost your productivity and efficiency. While there are countless options, focusing on a few key tools will help you build a strong foundation in an AI-driven environment. Beyond ChatGPT, explore other AI tools that perform similar functions but also have unique features tailored to specific tasks. For instance, some tools specialize in data analysis, project management or creative brainstorming, which might align better with your role or task requirements. Experimenting with different tools allows you to see what works best for each context.

Remember that the goal isn't to master every tool available – that could quickly become overwhelming. Instead, prioritize tools that truly simplify and speed up your workflow. Ask yourself, 'Is this making my life better, faster and simpler?' If the answer is yes, then keep adding more AI tools to your life and work until the opposite is true. This approach enables you to gradually incorporate more tools as needed to enhance your skills and adapt to evolving technology without feeling overloaded.

Perplexity.ai

Perplexity.ai is an AI-powered search engine that enhances your research capabilities. Unlike traditional search engines, it synthesizes information from multiple sources to provide comprehensive answers to your queries. For instance, if you're researching market trends in your industry, you can ask a complex question and Perplexity will compile insights from various credible sources, giving you a more holistic view than a standard search would.

Jasper

Jasper is another AI writing assistant that excels at content creation. Whether you need blog posts, ad copy or social media updates, Jasper can generate engaging content quickly. You can start with a brief description of what you want, and Jasper will provide several variations, allowing you to pick and edit the best fit. This is especially valuable for marketers looking to streamline their content strategy without compromising on quality.

Notion AI

Notion is a productivity tool that incorporates AI to help you organize your tasks and projects more efficiently. Notion AI allows you to generate summaries of meeting notes, create to-do lists and even brainstorm ideas for projects. The intuitive interface combined with AI features makes it a powerful tool for teams looking to collaborate and stay organized.

WHAT DO I NEED TO KNOW TO BE MY BEST AT WORK?

In a rapidly evolving workplace driven by AI, several key skills and knowledge areas will help you thrive. Here's what you need to focus on to maximize your effectiveness at work.

Understanding AI fundamentals

Start by grasping the basic concepts of AI and its applications. Familiarize yourself with key terms such as machine learning, natural language processing and data analytics. An understanding of these concepts will enable you to engage meaningfully in conversations about AI and its implications for your role and organization.

Mastering prompting

A critical skill in leveraging AI tools is learning how to craft effective prompts. Prompt engineering involves framing your requests to AI tools or asking questions clearly and concisely to ensure you get the desired output. For instance, instead of asking ChatGPT, 'Tell me about marketing', try something more specific, such as 'What are five innovative marketing strategies for small businesses today?' The more specific your prompts, the more relevant and useful the AI's responses will be.

Developing data literacy

As AI becomes more prevalent, its ability to interpret and analyse data will become invaluable. Therefore it is crucial that you familiarize yourself with basic data concepts, such as understanding charts, graphs and key performance indicators. Data literacy allows you to critically evaluate the insights AI tools provide and to make informed decisions based on these data.

WHAT ARE THE KEY TERMS TO KNOW FOR CONVERSATIONS ABOUT AI?

As AI becomes more integrated into the workplace, an understanding of the key terminology will not only enhance your own knowledge but also help you engage in meaningful discussions with colleagues. Here are some essential terms to get you started.

Machine learning

Machine learning refers to a subset of AI that enables machines to learn from data and improve their performance over time without being explicitly programmed. For example, **Netflix** uses machine-learning algorithms to analyse user viewing habits and recommend shows and movies based on individual preferences.

Generative AI

Generative AI is a category of AI that creates new content based on existing data. Tools such as **DALL·E** can generate images from text prompts, while ChatGPT can produce coherent text passages. This technology is transforming creative industries by automating content creation processes.

Natural language processing

Natural language processing is AI's ability to understand, interpret and generate human language. For instance, AI chatbots use NLP to interpret customer queries and respond in a conversational manner, thereby enhancing customer support experiences.

Automation

Automation refers to the use of AI technologies to perform repetitive tasks with minimal human intervention. For instance, marketing automation tools can schedule social media posts, analyse campaign performance and send personalized emails to customers, thus freeing up time for marketing teams to focus on strategy.

Data privacy

Data privacy refers to the ethical and legal considerations regarding the handling of personal data. As AI systems often rely on vast amounts of data, understanding regulations such as the General Data Protection Regulation (GDPR) will help you navigate discussions around data usage and security in your organization.

HOW WILL AI AFFECT HOW I NAVIGATE WORK?

AI is poised to transform the workplace, and understanding its impact on navigation and workflows is crucial for adapting to it successfully. Here's how AI will influence your day-to-day operations.

Decision-making support

AI's data analysis capabilities will provide valuable insights that enhance decision making. For example, predictive analytics tools can analyse historical data to forecast sales trends or customer behaviour. This means you'll have data-driven insights at your fingertips, enabling you to make informed decisions rather than relying solely on gut feelings.

Personalized workflows

AI can help create personalized workflows tailored to your preferences and work style. For example, AI-driven project-management tools can suggest task prioritization based on your previous work habits, ensuring that you focus on what's most important. This level of personalization enhances productivity and satisfaction in your work.

Navigating challenges

AI can assist with identifying potential challenges before they escalate. For instance, in project management, AI tools can analyse project timelines and resource allocations to highlight areas at risk of delay. It will help you catch issues early, as you can proactively address them and maintain project momentum.

HOW WILL AI AFFECT HOW I LEAD?

As AI technology continues to permeate the workplace, the role of leaders will evolve in significant ways. Here's how AI will influence leadership styles and practices.

Embracing technology

Leaders will need to become advocates for AI adoption within their teams. This means understanding the tools available and their potential benefits. For instance, leaders who promote AI-powered analytics tools can help their teams make data-driven decisions rather than relying solely on intuition. By embracing technology, leaders can create a culture that values innovation and efficiency.

Empowering teams

AI enables leaders to empower their teams by automating routine tasks to allow employees to focus on strategic initiatives and creative problem solving. For example, if a team spends considerable time on administrative tasks, leaders can implement AI tools to automate those processes, thus freeing up time for higher-level work. This empowerment fosters engagement and encourages team members to take ownership of their projects.

Promoting continuous learning

As AI technology evolves, leaders must foster a culture of continuous learning. Encourage team members to experiment with AI tools, attend workshops and share their insights. For example, implementing 'AI Fridays', where team members dedicate time to explore new AI applications or share what they've learnt, can promote a learning mindset. Leaders who prioritize learning will help their teams adapt to rapid technological changes.

Leveraging data for strategy

AI provides leaders with access to data-driven insights that can inform strategic decisions. For example, the use of predictive analytics can help leaders forecast market trends or customer behaviours. Insights related to these analytics allow leaders to make informed decisions about product development, marketing strategies and resource allocation. Leaders who leverage data can position their organizations for success in an increasingly competitive landscape.

HOW WILL AI AFFECT HOW I THINK AND DECIDE?

As AI continues to evolve and integrate into everyday business practices, it will fundamentally change the way you think and make decisions. Here's how.

Scenario planning

AI can help you think through various scenarios and their potential outcomes. By modelling different possibilities based on historical data, AI can provide insights into potential future trends. For example, if you're considering launching a new product, AI tools can analyse market conditions, customer preferences and competitor activity to project likely success rates. This scenario planning allows for more informed and strategic decision making.

Enhanced problem solving

AI can serve as a powerful brainstorming partner. When faced with a complex problem, you can use AI tools to generate a variety of potential solutions or approaches. For instance, AI-driven platforms can analyse previous case studies to suggest strategies that have worked in similar situations. This enhances your problem-solving capabilities by expanding your options and fostering creative thinking.

Recognizing bias

As AI systems can carry inherent biases based on the data they're trained on, it's essential for you to remain vigilant about potential biases in decision making. Understanding how AI algorithms work will help you critically assess their recommendations and outcomes. For example, if an AI tool suggests a specific candidate for a job based on biased historical data, recognizing this bias can lead you to conduct further evaluations to ensure fair hiring practices.

Ethical considerations

As you incorporate AI into your decision making, ethical considerations will become increasingly important. Questions surrounding data privacy, consent and transparency must be at the forefront of your thought process. For example, if an AI tool uses customer data for analysis, it's vital to ensure that all such data is collected ethically and handled in a way that complies with regulations. Ethically sound decisions will enhance your credibility and build trust within your organization.

WHAT ARE THE BASICS OF PROMPT ENGINEERING?

Prompt engineering is the process of designing and refining input prompts to guide AI systems, especially language models, to produce accurate, relevant and high-quality responses. A prompt serves as the question or instruction given to the AI, and how you craft it influences the AI's output significantly. This skill is crucial, because a well-constructed prompt ensures a more reliable answer, enhances productivity and reduces misinterpretation. In business, effective prompts help companies extract insights, generate content and streamline decision making. If you were a five-year-old, we'd explain prompt engineering like this (this is the new answer I got when I asked ChatGPT this question after it provided the answer above: 'Please provide this explanation to me again like I am a five-year-old'):

> Imagine you're telling a smart robot what to do, like giving it step-by-step instructions to build a Lego castle. When you tell it exactly what you want, it does a great job. But if you're unclear, it might build something that doesn't look like a castle at all. Prompt engineering is like learning how to ask really good questions so the robot (or AI) can give you the best answers possible. In a business, people use these questions, or 'prompts', to ask the AI things like, 'What do customers like best?' or 'Give me ideas for a fun new toy!' When prompts are clear and well-thought-out, the robot's answers help people

make smarter choices, write better messages, or come up with great ideas faster.

Prompt engineering generally involves the following:
- **Setting clear goals**: Defining the purpose of the prompt (for example, content creation, idea generation and customer support).
- **Specifying details**: These include relevant context, details or format instructions in the prompt to guide responses.
- **Iterative refinement**: Testing and adjusting prompts to improve accuracy and relevance in output.

Some basic business prompts
- **Market analysis**: 'What are the current trends in the [industry name] market for [year]?'
- **Competitor overview**: 'Summarize the strengths and weaknesses of [competitor's name] in the [specific area].'
- **Customer persona**: 'Describe a detailed customer persona for a [product/service]. Include demographics, needs and purchasing behaviour.'
- **Content idea generation**: 'List five blog post ideas about [topic].'
- **Email response assistance**: 'Provide a polite response to a client asking about delays in project delivery.'

Intermediate business prompts
- **Customer pain points analysis**: 'Identify three common pain points customers face when using [type of product/service].'
- **Brand tone creation**: 'Create a brand tone and voice guide for a company that is [add adjectives, for example innovative, friendly]. Provide example phrases.'
- **Competitor differentiation strategy**: 'List three ways

[company name] can differentiate itself from [competitor] in the [specific market].'

- **Product feature prioritization**: 'Suggest the top five features to prioritize for a new [type of product] targeted at [specific customer segment].'
- **Marketing campaign ideas**: 'Generate three creative campaign ideas for launching [product/service]. Specify target audience and provide key messages.'

Advanced business prompts

- **Predictive market changes**: 'Analyse [industry] trends and suggest potential shifts over the next five years. Include opportunities and risks.'
- **Competitive landscape analysis**: 'Assess the competitive landscape for [company name] and suggest three unique market entry strategies for [new market/country].'
- **Cross-industry innovation ideas**: 'Generate ideas for applying successful strategies from the [other industry] to [target industry]. Explain the rationale.'
- **Complex problem solving**: 'Propose a three-step solution to tackle the issue of [specific challenge, for example low user engagement] for [company name]. Include examples of similar successful strategies.'
- **Customer journey mapping**: 'Describe a comprehensive customer journey map for a high-end [product/service]. Include stages, emotions and touchpoints.'

Effective use of these prompts involves iterating and adapting them based on results. Over time, understanding how to design prompts can help you get more nuanced and targeted information from AI, which can greatly enhance efficiency and insight in business decision making.

HOW TO USE CHATGPT
LIKE A STRATEGIC GENIUS

Since ChatGPT is used for problem solving, and most of business and life is problem solving, it would make sense to learn how to use ChatGPT and other generative AI tools like some of the best problem solvers out there. McKinsey consultants are known to be some of the best at problem solving and presenting strategic solutions in business, and, until now, you had to vigorously learn how to think like them to apply their mental prowess to your own business questions. But now you can simply ask ChatGPT to answer your business questions like a McKinsey consultant. ChatGPT, like Google, has scoured the entire web and learnt from all the existing resources on how to think like one. Now you can use it to produce answers in the same style that they would. This is true for any type of thinking or style of problem solving in business, science, engineering and creativity – McKinsey is only one example. But we can now learn to think like the world's best, or at least ask ChatGPT to think like the world's best for us.

To use ChatGPT like a McKinsey analyst, you'll want to focus on three main areas: data-driven analysis, strategic insights and structured, concise communication. Here's how you can leverage ChatGPT effectively to mimic this type of high-level consulting approach.

Data-driven analysis and synthesis

- **Ask ChatGPT for summaries and trends:** Instead of manually sifting through data or articles, prompt ChatGPT to summarize the latest trends, key industry statistics or competitive insights in a specific industry or market. For example: 'What are the current trends in the renewable energy sector, focusing on innovation, investment and regulatory shifts?'

- **Scenario analysis**: ChatGPT can help explore potential outcomes for a business problem by creating different scenarios. Try prompts such as: 'Create three scenarios for how AI adoption might affect the retail industry over the next five years.' This approach is similar to the scenario planning that consultants often use to assess risks and opportunities.
- **Identify key metrics and KPIs**: Ask ChatGPT to list metrics relevant to specific objectives that are foundational for evaluating business strategies. For example: 'List the KPIs for assessing supply chain efficiency in the manufacturing industry.'

Strategic insights and business frameworks

- **Use consulting frameworks**: You can prompt ChatGPT to think in terms of popular consulting frameworks such as SWOT (strengths, weaknesses, opportunities, threats) analysis, Porter's Five Forces or the 3C model (customers, competitors, company). For instance: 'Conduct a SWOT analysis for a new product launch in the telecommunications industry.'
- **PESTLE analysis**: To understand macroeconomic factors, ask ChatGPT to perform a PESTLE analysis, which includes political, economic, social, technological, legal and environmental factors. This can be particularly useful when assessing market entry strategies.
- **Formulating hypotheses**: Use ChatGPT to craft hypotheses based on business issues. For instance: 'Formulate three hypotheses on why our customer churn rate has increased in the past quarter.' This gives you a structured way to start investigating the problem, similar to what a consultant would come up with.

Concise, structured communication

- **Executive summaries**: ChatGPT can help you create concise, executive-level summaries. Try prompts such as: 'Summarize key insights for an executive presentation on the impact of remote work in tech companies.'
- **Problem-driven structure**: Consultants often use a mutually exclusive, collectively exhaustive (MECE) structure to break down complex problems into distinct categories. Ask ChatGPT: 'Present an MECE framework for addressing declining sales in the consumer electronics sector.'
- **Drafting recommendations**: After gathering insights, ChatGPT can assist in formulating recommendations. For example: 'Based on the identified issues, provide three actionable recommendations to improve employee retention in a high-turnover industry.'

Sample prompts for advanced analysis

- **Basic prompts:**
  - 'What are the key growth trends in the digital healthcare industry?'
  - 'Summarize the competitive landscape for the cloud computing market.'
  - 'Provide a list of KPIs for evaluating customer satisfaction in the hospitality sector.'
  - 'Explain the benefits and drawbacks of a direct-to-consumer business model.'
  - 'Identify recent innovations in the logistics industry.'
- **Intermediate prompts:**
  - 'Conduct a PESTLE analysis for the electric vehicle industry in Europe.'
  - 'List strategic risks and mitigation strategies for retail expansion into Asia.'

- 'Outline a customer segmentation approach for a financial services company targeting millennials.'
- 'Draft a SWOT analysis for a startup in the renewable energy sector.'
- 'Propose three growth strategies for an e-commerce company facing high competition.'

- **Advanced prompts:**
  - 'Develop three strategic scenarios for how AI might transform the insurance industry over the next decade.'
  - 'Create a Porter's Five Forces analysis for a new entrant in the mobile banking space.'
  - 'Formulate hypotheses for why a subscription-based SaaS company is seeing declining renewal rates.'
  - 'Recommend a digital transformation roadmap for a traditional retail brand, focusing on e-commerce and data analytics.'
  - 'Outline an MECE framework for addressing supply chain inefficiencies in a multinational manufacturing firm.'

HOW TO USE CHATGPT TO THINK BIGGER, LIKE SIMON SINEK

McKinsey's problem-solving frameworks can also be considered mental models, and a mental model is a simplified way of understanding complex concepts or systems by breaking them down into more manageable, relatable frameworks. Mental models are tools that help people think through problems, make decisions and understand how different elements interact within a system. They're widely used in business, science, psychology and everyday life to solve problems and make effective decisions by providing a structured way of thinking.

For example, a common mental model is 'first principles

thinking', which involves reducing a problem to its core components to find innovative solutions. Another is 'opportunity cost', which helps people understand that choosing one action often means forgoing another potential gain. While ChatGPT may not always be perfect at analysing the world through these models, it can provide incredible insights to enhance or inspire your thinking. Simon Sinek's mental models, particularly his focus on 'finding your "why"', 'circle of safety' and 'infinite mindset', are powerful frameworks for using ChatGPT to guide business thinking, leadership and personal growth. Here's how to apply ChatGPT with these models to get insightful and relevant answers.

Finding your 'why'

- **How it works**: Sinek's 'start with why' model centres on discovering and articulating the core purpose behind actions, businesses or products.
- **How to use ChatGPT**: Start by asking ChatGPT to help brainstorm or refine your 'why' by framing prompts that clarify purpose.
  - **Example prompt**: 'Use Simon Sinek's philosophy "start with why" to help me articulate the "why" of our company's mission, focusing on how we create value beyond profits.'
- **Outcome**: ChatGPT can help generate language and ideas that clarify the purpose of your organization or personal mission, thereby encouraging deeper alignment with Sinek's focus on authenticity.

Circle of safety

- **How it works**: This model promotes creating a safe and inclusive environment in which team members feel protected

and supported, which Sinek suggests is essential for trust and collaboration.
- **How to use ChatGPT**: You can ask ChatGPT for strategies to foster a 'circle of safety' in your organization.
  - Example prompt: 'Inspired by Sinek's "circle of safety", suggest strategies to enhance team trust and build a "circle of safety" in our remote work culture.'
- **Outcome**: ChatGPT can provide ideas and best practices for establishing trust and psychological safety within teams, such as developing empathetic leadership skills or creating transparent communication channels.

Infinite mindset
- **How it works**: Sinek's 'infinite mindset' encourages focusing on long-term vision rather than short-term wins by advocating for adaptability, resilience and purpose-driven work.
- **How to use ChatGPT**: Request assistance with applying an 'infinite mindset' to business strategy or career development.
  - Example prompt: 'Based on Sinek's "infinite mindset" theory, help me create a long-term strategy that supports sustainable growth and aligns with an "infinite mindset".'
- **Outcome**: ChatGPT can provide a list of principles and strategies focused on resilience, adaptability and purpose, such as investing in relationships or aligning goals with long-term values over quarterly results.

HOW TO USE CHATGPT TO THINK LIKE A CREATIVE BRAIN

To boost creativity using ChatGPT, you can apply several mental models that help shape your thinking. Here are some powerful models with prompts to guide your creative process.

First principles thinking (used by Elon Musk)

The model for first principles thinking involves breaking down complex ideas into their basic core elements. To apply this in ChatGPT, you could ask it the following:

- 'What are the basic principles or core needs behind this problem/idea?'
- 'What assumptions am I making about this idea, and how can I challenge them?'

By stripping away assumptions, you can uncover new ways to approach a challenge. For instance, if you're designing a product, ask ChatGPT: 'What is the absolute essence of what this product must do?' This can lead to innovative, foundational ideas.

Inversion (used by Charlie Munger)

Think about the opposite of your goal to find new solutions. For creativity, you can use ChatGPT to explore what would make your idea fail. Prompts include:

- 'What would cause this idea/product to fail?'
- 'How could I make this situation worse, and why would that happen?'

This type of thinking helps identify hidden risks and challenges while opening the door to new, more effective ideas.

SCAMPER (used by Kellogg's)

The SCAMPER method focuses on creative problem solving by modifying existing concepts. Use ChatGPT to explore each SCAMPER strategy.

- **Substitute:** 'What can I replace in this product/service to make it more effective?'

- **Combine**: 'How could I combine two existing ideas into something new?'
- **Adapt**: 'How could I adapt this concept for a different industry?'
- **Modify**: 'What can I modify in this idea to improve it?'
- **Put to another use**: 'What other uses can I find for this product?'
- **Eliminate**: 'What features can I remove to make this product simpler or more efficient?'
- **Reverse**: 'What would happen if I reversed the order or approach to this idea?'

These prompts can help you explore various ways to innovate or tweak ideas for a fresh perspective.

The Feynman technique (used by Bill Gates)

The Feynman technique involves simplifying complex concepts by explaining them as if teaching someone else. Use ChatGPT to break down and clarify complex ideas by asking it:

- 'Explain this concept to a five-year-old.'
- 'Can you simplify this explanation so even a beginner could understand it?'

By rephrasing complicated ideas, you often gain new insights and uncover innovative ways to approach a problem.

Mental simulation (used by superforecasters)

The model for mental simulation encourages imagining different outcomes based on specific actions. You can use ChatGPT to simulate possible futures by asking:

- 'If I take this action, what might happen in the next month?'
- 'What are three possible outcomes if I adjust this business strategy?'

Mental simulation with ChatGPT helps you visualize diverse possibilities, making it easier to brainstorm multiple solutions and choose the most effective one.

MINDSET FOR THE WAY FORWARD

What you can see is that the abundant future comes not only from abundance of information but from the abundant ways in which that information can be organized. This means anyone, anywhere, can think like a billionaire CEO, a Nobel Prize scientist or a creative genius. It is true that many beautiful things in this world come from our intuition and ability to observe the world and find little details that others do not notice, but combining that with the computing power of AI to generate new solutions or create new workflows makes us virtually unstoppable. In a future where you can create anything, the only question is what will that be?

Having said that, the world will feel like a very noisy and overwhelming space for the next decade, but no matter how many tools or technologies or courses or ideas compete for our attention, we will never truly be in a rush to capture some temporary gold. We have infinite time, and as more jobs get swallowed up, many more opportunities will become available. So while you need to actively participate in this new world, do not be in a rush to understand and grasp it all at once. Like you, billions more are now making the journey. And like you, billions more stand to win from the billions more. This is truly the most exciting time in history, and you're living it right now. So keep your ear to the ground, learn as much as you can and enjoy the ride.